Game ON!

Game ON!

Nine Sports Shorts

LEN SPACEK

ISBN: 978-0-578-42974-8

Library of Congress Control Number: 2018966784

Champion Performance & Counseling LLC.
Cleveland, Ohio

For the athletes and students whom have made a difference in my life.

I hope this book will make a difference in yours.

Karen –
Do what's right!
Do your best!
Don't ever give up!!

J. M. Smith

"It is not the critic who counts; not the man who points out how the strong man stumbles or where the doer of deeds could have done them better. The credit belongs to the man who is actually in the arena, whose face is marred by dust and sweat and blood, who strives valiantly, who errs and comes up short again and again, because there is no effort without error or shortcoming. It is the man who strives to do the deeds, who knows the great enthusiasms, the great devotions, who spends himself in a worthy cause; who, at the best, knows, in the end, the triumph of high achievement, and who, at the worst, if he fails, at least he fails while daring greatly, so that his place shall never be with those cold and timid souls who neither know victory nor defeat."

—Theodore Roosevelt

CONTENTS

FALL

SOCCER: SUAH'S WAY

"Every kid around the world who plays soccer wants to be Pelé. I have a great responsibility to show them not just how to be like a soccer player, but how to be like a man."

—Pelé
(Professional Soccer Player)

Navy blue and white fill the side of the stadium of the Rootstown Rovers. On our side of the stadium, the stands are overflowing with the black and gold of the Garrettsville G-men. When the game ends in a 0-0 tie, we go to a sudden death shoot-out. The first six kicks find the back of the net to tie the game at 3-3. Rootstown scores on the next kick. When I step up for my kick, we are down four to three. My goal can tie the game. If we win this game, then we advance in the state tournament, and the Rovers go home. Their season will be over.

The referee spots the ball on the circle in front of the net. Looking at the goalie, I know that he has to guess where my kick will go. If you kick the ball in the right place, it's almost impossible to react in time to make the save. The goalie must anticipate your kick. There is no room for error.

Their goalie is short and stocky and his eyes seem to be glazed over. It's obvious that the pressure has gotten to him. He has already let three goals go by, and he's looking less and less confident. He is bent over, hands on knees, and breathing hard.

My teammates cheer me on. "Come on, Patrick!"

"One time!"

"You can do it!"

Approaching the ball, I keep my head down and accelerate my foot through the ball. It takes flight, like a missile, toward the upper left hand corner of the goal. Even though the goalie guesses right, the kick is perfect, and he doesn't even manage to get a hand on it. The ball catches and spins in the upper corner of the net. The fans on our side of the packed stadium cheer, wave towels, and shake jars filled with pennies. We are tied 4-4.

Jogging back to the sideline, I approach our goalie, Jason Adkins. "One stop is all we need," I tell him. "Suah will win it for us on his kick."

Jason, who is all of six foot four, gives me a high five as he takes his position in front of the goal. He wears his bright yellow goalie shirt, and a look of unshakeable confidence.

The kid from Rootstown that steps up for their final sudden-death kick is their best player. He eyes the ball and searches the goal for his sweet spot. Coach has scouted the Rovers, knows that this player likes to hook the ball and will shoot for the left corner of the goal. Jason knows this, so he cheats to his left, giving their player a wider target, and a false sense of hope. With Jason's long wingspan, he will easily make up the distance.

The player approaches the ball, and Jason immediately breaks to his right, toward the corner of the goal. Before the player realizes that he needs to change the direction of his kick, it's too late. His kick takes flight without much punch.

Jason dives to his left, and just as the ball is about to break the plane of the goal, he bats the ball away, and it rolls out of bounds. Our fans go crazy, knowing it will all come down to the final kick in sudden-death overtime.

This leaves it up to Suah. With one kick, he can win the game. Suah, who is an exchange student from Liberia, has the chance to be the hero of our school with one shot on goal. Suah is short with powerful legs. He is strong and fast, as if he were born to play soccer. Sometimes it seems like the ball is just an extension of his body. He's that good.

Suah gives me a high five as he jogs toward the ball. His high five smacks my hand; he is filled with energy. Right then, I get this overwhelming feeling that his kick is going to go in, and it will be the first year our school has advanced this far into the state tournament. After the referee blows the whistle, Suah sprints toward the ball without hesitation. The ball rockets off Suah's foot and sails high and to the right side of the goal. The goalie reacts quickly and dives to his left, actually getting a hand on the ball, but because the kick is so powerful, it glances off the gloves of the goalie and spins in the back of the net. Suah has won the game for us. Our team jumps in celebration, and we sprint toward Suah. He raises his hands briefly in victory. Humility is Suah's way. Soon after, our entire team mobs him. We all hug Suah and give him high fives.

Suah closes his eyes, and a giant smile spreads across his face. He is the hero. The Garrettsville G-men will continue to advance in this year's state soccer tournament.

In the locker room after the game, Jason says, "Party tonight at my house. Parents are out of town for the weekend."

I look at Suah and ask, "Want to go?"

"Sure, Patrick," he says.

"Cool. I'll pick you up around eight."

Later that night, my five speed Volkswagen Jetta cruises down Main Street in the center of town. We blare the music, feeling invincible and on top of the world.

Jason's house is tucked in the very back of the development, far enough away from the other houses that hopefully nobody will call the cops. When we get to the house, Jason meets us at the front door. He fills the entire doorway.

"Welcome!" he shouts over the pounding of the house music. "Kegs are on the back porch!" He gives me and Suah fist bumps, and says, "Bonfire starts at ten."

"Nice," I say, "just like we used to."

Jason smiles and says, "I even bought some marshmallows."

In the house, players from the soccer team are everywhere with some girls and some other friends from school. A group of guys from our school are playing a drinking game at the kitchen table.

At the keg on the back porch, two players from our team are drinking. I turn to Suah and ask, "Do you drink?"

"No," he says. "I don't."

"Neither do I," I say. Thinking about the commitment we all made to the team, I am disappointed by some of the other players on our team who are drinking.

Soon the party is roaring. Jason is playing DJ, spinning some Jay Z song. Guys and girls are talking above the music and drinking. After a while, I notice that Suah is not around. I search the house, wondering where he could have gone. Finally, I find him in the backyard, by himself, working on getting the bonfire started.

"What are you doing out here?" I ask.

"The party is too loud for me. I like the quiet back here," he says.

"I understand," I say, as I help Suah by gathering some sticks in the woods and getting some logs from the pile on the side of the house.

Suah stacks the wood on the fire in the shape of a teepee and says, "When I was little, we would make a fire every night in our yard. We had an old stone oven. My grandma would bake fresh bread. She would make homemade butter." Suah smiles to himself and says, "You've never tasted anything like my grandma's bread with homemade butter. It's like heaven." Suah gets a look on his face like he's enjoying some of that homemade butter right now.

"I bet that butter was good." Looking at Suah, I ask, "Do you miss being home?"

"A little bit," Suah says with a trace of an accent. "I miss my family."

"What do you like best about being here?" I ask.

Suah gets a look of satisfaction on his face. "I love playing soccer. It's been great being on this team. The whole town has embraced me. In many ways, I feel like I have made a new home here."

"You won the game for us today," I say.

Suah folds up some newspapers and puts them under the sticks and logs that we have gathered. Shaking his head, he says, "No, it was a team effort. Everybody was a part of the win today."

"We wouldn't have nearly as good of a team without you," I say, handing Suah a match that Jason gave me from his fireplace.

"That's nice of you to say, but I don't know if it's true. This is a good team you have here." He takes the match and strikes it on a rock. Walking around the logs, he carefully lights each newspaper, and slowly, the fire begins to burn.

"Coach Riley must have a lot of confidence in you. He put you as the last man in the shootout. If that isn't pure trust, I don't know what is."

Suah shrugs his shoulders, and shaking off the compliment, he changes the subject. "When I got here, I didn't know anybody except for the family that I'm living with... and you. You showed me to my classes and sat with me at lunch. Why did you do that?"

I want to tell Suah that's the kind of person I am, that people in our town are just that way. But instead, I tell him the truth. "Coach Riley asked me to take you around. He asked me to eat lunch with you the first week or so, until you felt comfortable."

Suah drops his head. "Oh," he says, "I didn't mean to be a burden for you. I hope I wasn't an inconvenience."

I wave him off. "Please don't think that. I'm glad that Coach asked me. I'm glad I was the one he picked. I like you Suah. I think you're a cool kid. I feel like I've made a new friend."

"Me, too," says Suah, as he grabs a couple more logs and adds them to the fire. Using a long stick, he repositions the other logs on the fire to make it burn better. Soon the flames are dancing into the night. Suah takes a seat next to me on the bench. For a long while, Suah and I stare into the fire that continues to grow in size and strength. The smell from the smoke and the burning wood makes me think about camping with my family. I start to think about my parents, and how they are getting divorced. I consider how this announcement came out of the blue. It was something I never anticipated or expected. My parents argue like most parents, but I had no idea it had gotten so bad.

Suah must notice something is bothering me because he asks, "Patrick, are you okay?"

"Yeah, I'm fine," I say.

"What are you thinking about?" he asks knowingly. "You seem to be staring off."

Letting out a deep breath, I say, "It's about my parents. They're getting divorced. Things have been tough around the house. My dad is always on edge, and my mom is having a really tough time dealing with all of it."

"I'm sorry to hear that," says Suah. "Is there anything I can do to help you?"

"No, but thanks," I say, continuing to stare into the fire, thinking about how my family is slowly falling apart. I think about the fact that I am only one year away from graduation and how my little brother will have to deal with the divorce more than me once I leave for college.

"Patrick," Suah says, interrupting my thoughts, "everybody deals with something at different times in their life."

"Yeah, I know. It's just been tough. You know."

Suah says, "Patrick, can I tell you something about me?"

"Sure, go ahead," I say, wondering what Suah could possibly say to top the divorce of my parents.

Suah shifts uncomfortably, like he's preparing for some big unveiling. "I'm not an exchange student.

I'm here because of Unicef. I was adopted by the Sylvan family."

"Really?" I ask, wondering why Suah would have been adopted.

Suah gets a pained look on his face and says, "My family was killed by rebel soldiers in Liberia."

I push back in my chair. This information has packed a punch. "What are you talking about? I thought you were an exchange student. That..."

Suah interrupts me and says, "I became a soldier when I was twelve years old."

Suddenly the divorce of my parents doesn't seem so big. In fact, my problems are dwarfed. Looking at Suah, I say, "A soldier?"

Suah nods his head. "Yes, a soldier. I chose to fight against the rebel army."

"You were in a war?" I shake my head in disbelief. "You're only sixteen, and you've been in a war?"

Suah looks down and says, "I've done some horrible things, Patrick. Sometimes, I feel ugly inside for the things I have seen, and the things I have done. Sometimes, I feel ugly, inside and out."

I have to catch my breath. "How long were you a soldier?"

Anguish fills Suah's face. "I fought for two years. Two very long years."

I'm not sure if it is my place to ask, but my curiosity gets the best of me. I don't want to offend Suah or be insensitive, but I want to know all about Suah and what he went through. "What happened?" I ask.

Suah looks hard into the fire. "I've done some things I am not proud of. I was so angry for what happened to my family that I did things I never knew I was capable of doing."

I feel a lump in my throat. Stories like these never come to the small town of Garrettsville. "You've killed people?"

Suah nods his head, and without showing any real emotion, he says, "Yes."

I've never been afraid of Suah, but this new information has put me on my guard. And despite my new feeling toward Suah, I want to know more. "What was it like... to kill someone?" I ask.

Suah shudders for a moment, and then he composes himself. "It felt... horrible... and good, all at the same time. Revenge was good, initially. But then what I had done began to sink in, and I couldn't get it out of my head." Suah is quiet for a long moment and then says, "I have nightmares. I wake up in a cold sweat most nights, thinking about the things I have done. Some of the dreams are so real. I can see the blood, hear the AK-47, and feel my heart racing. It's like living the horror over and over again."

"How did you survive? How did you make it out of there?" I ask.

"The Sylvan family adopted me when I was fifteen years old, and I moved to the United States."

Looking at Suah, I wonder how he could have fought in a war at such a young age, and how he had actually killed rebel soldiers. Looking into the fire, I ask, "How do you deal with the loss of your family?"

"Forgiveness," says Suah, without missing a beat, "forgiveness for the people who took the lives of my family. This was not easy. My mother. My father. My older brother. They were all taken from me."

I think about my mom and dad. And then I think about my little brother. The divorce is one thing, but I couldn't even imagine losing my family like Suah has. I don't know how I would feel. Probably the same rage and anger that Suah felt. I would want the same revenge. Looking at Suah, I wonder how he could ever find that kind of compassion to forgive the rebel army for what they had done to his family. "How did you find the strength to forgive the people who killed your family?"

I can see the strain on his face. "It wasn't easy," he says. "But do you know what was even harder?" he asks.

"What's that?" I say, wondering what could possibly be harder than forgiving the people who killed your family.

"The hardest thing I've learned is to forgive myself for the things I have done. The horrible things I have done." He pauses for a long minute and then asks, "Isn't that strange?"

"You did what anyone would have done. You defended yourself and you got revenge for your family." Standing up, I use a stick to rearrange some of the logs on the fire. It is now blazing. Looking back at Suah, I ask, "How did you eventually forgive yourself?"

"I've been counseled for a long time, almost two years now. The Sylvan family has helped me more than I could have asked for. And of course, there's soccer."

"Soccer?"

A smile lights up Suah's face. "I've been play-ing soccer ever since I can remember. Since I started walking, I always had a soccer ball at my feet, but this was the first year I was able to play for a school. Up until now, I wasn't ready to be around other people. I feel lucky to be here." The light from the fire fills Suah's face.

"How did soccer help you?"

"Before I joined school, I had almost a full school year on my own. I would go up to the abandoned brick building behind the high school and kick the ball against the wall, over and over. I made my left leg just as strong as my right. The repetition of kicking that ball over and over again was my best therapy. I would just kick the ball, and run through the things in my life. The repetition of kicking the ball and the repetition of going through the pain that I experienced in the war helped me get through it. My counselor told me not to go around the pain. Go through it. I face it and go through it every day. It allows me to heal."

I look over at Suah and ask, "Is that why you're so good?"

Suah shakes his head. "I don't believe that I'm good."

Suah is the most humble person I know.

"You're the best player on our team, and usually, you're the best player on the field when we play an-other team."

A small smile appears on Suah's face. "Do you know what motivates me?"

"What?" I ask.

"The memory of my family. I dedicate every game to my family. My father and mother, and my brother, they are my motivation. They are my passion. It's not about winning or losing for me. It's not about the school. It's about honoring my family."

I try to take in all that Suah has said. It all seems so unreal, so hard to believe. I can't even begin to comprehend the idea that someone my age has gone through something so awful and seen all the things that he has. Looking at Suah in a much different way, I ask, "And that has made you into the player that you are today?"

Suah says, "Whenever I score a goal, and the team hugs me and celebrates with me, I close my eyes and pretend the embrace is from my family. That is what drives me." Suah closes his eyes.

Maybe he is picturing his family.

I put another log on the fire, just as a few guys from the team walk out of Jason's house.

"Good job on the fire, boys!" calls Jason from the house.

Suah looks at me and says, "Patrick, what I have said was only meant for you. You are my only good friend here. I don't want anyone else to know."

I nod my head. "Of course," I say. Then I add, "I haven't told anyone about my parents getting divorced. Would you keep that between us?"

"Of course, Patrick." Suah stands up and says, "Thank you for all you've done. You are a good friend."

Shrugging my shoulders, I say, "I don't think I've done anything."

"You've been my friend. That is worth more than anything in the world. That is something you cannot put a price on. You've done more than you will ever know, just by being my friend."

While the guys from the team look for sticks in the woods, Jason breaks out the marshmallows. I sit by the fire and think about my parents getting divorced, and then I think about Suah losing his family. I think about what Suah said about how important my friendship has been to him. And suddenly, my problems don't seem so big anymore. And more importantly, I think about how important Suah's friendship is to me.

Jason slides a marshmallow on the end of a stick and says, "A great fire, a winning soccer season, and marshmallows… what could be better?"

As I sit with Suah next to that fire, I think about everything he has been through, and then I consider all the things in my life that I have taken for granted.

Later that night, I drive Suah back to his house, the Sylvan's. On the way there, he asks, "Do you know what Suah means?"

"No idea," I say, turning down the radio.

Suah points his finger in the air and says, "It means a new beginning."

"That's cool. What do you think your new beginning will be?" I ask.

"I'm not sure, but I know that I have a chance to start over. Start a family of my own, here in America.

A family that will never see the things I have seen in Liberia. Starting a family here in America is one of my dreams. It would be the greatest gift that I could give to the memory of my father, my mother, and my brother."

Turning down the Sylvan's street, I look at him and say, "It will happen for you one day."

"Do you know what else I want more than anything?" Suah says.

"What's that?" I ask.

"I want to be a professional soccer player," he says.

Pulling into Suah's driveway, I say, "If anybody can go pro, it's you." I put the car in park.

Suah is too humble to say that he knows this is true. He is quiet for a moment. As he reaches for the handle on the door, he says, "So, we have our next tournament game on Monday."

"Yeah, I can't wait. It's the first time our school has ever made it this far into the playoffs. Are you excited for the next game?"

Suah nods his head and smiles broadly. "It's what I live for."

Driving home, I think about what soccer has given to Suah. For Suah, soccer is more than just a game. Soccer is more than the opportunity to match his skills with other athletes. For Suah, soccer is a way to heal from all the horrible things that have happened to him. Soccer was his way of dealing with the pain. It was his way of escaping, just long enough to get through the mess, and a way to get back to living. I never considered soccer being anything more than a game. But now, I do. Maybe, just maybe, soccer can help me get through my parents' divorce. And of course my friends from the team will help. They have always been there for me, including Suah. As I pull in my driveway, I think about Suah, and I know that if he can get through losing his family, I can get through the divorce of my parents. In fact, I can get through anything.

After a weekend filled with the anticipation of our next tournament game, and the continued fighting of my parents, Monday finally arrives. On the bus ride to the game, I sit with Suah. We talk soccer strategy and school. He tells me more about his life in Liberia, about his mom and dad, and his brother. How he was one of only ten people to survive the attack on his village.

Suah says, "You know the people with Unicef really helped me. One of the counselors told me that my view of the world would always depend on me. I have the opportunity to view my past as something horrible, or I can view it as something I had tremendous courage to survive and overcome. That message will always remain with me."

"It's an unbelievable story. You are lucky to have made it out of Liberia, and here you are with us."

Suah nods his head and says, "I have the chance to write a new story now. I can write my story the way that I would like to see it play out."

More and more I admire Suah for who he is and his courage. Listening to Suah gives me the courage to do the things he has done to survive.

Suah interrupts my thoughts when he says, "My brother was a better soccer player than I am."

Shaking my head, I say, "I don't believe it."

"Yes, it's true. He taught me how to play. He taught me the bicycle kick. Like Pelé."

"You can do that?" I ask.

Suah shrugs his shoulders and smiles. "The timing has to be perfect. The situation has to be perfect. But yes, I can do it."

When the bus rolls into the parking lot and the brakes squeak the bus to a stop, I look at Suah and say, "I would love to see that."

Suah laughs and says, "Me, too."

We take the field and warm up. The adrenaline flows through my body. During the warm up, I look at Suah and think about what he said about not especially caring about winning or losing, how he plays for the honor of his family. I've never thought about what I played for. It was always just to play for my school, to win for my friends. When I think about Suah, I realize that his passion for the game runs deeper than mine or the other players on our team. But I know that now, I will play for something more than my school. I will play for Suah.

The stadium is filled with fans. We warm up on the field, stretching, and taking shots on goal. The team from Canton hasn't lost a game all season. But Suah's story has given me a passion I have not felt before. If he could do the things he has done, I can find the courage to face this team on this day.

Soon, we are ready to play.

When the referee blows the whistle, I get the opening pass from Suah. I dribble the ball through the first line of defense. I quickly pass the ball back to Suah on the right wing. Suah maneuvers the ball through the second line of defense, until he is one-on-one with their goalie.

Suah moves differently from the other players. It's an effortless fluidity. He shoots the ball at the goal, but the goalie manages to deflect the ball. The ball shoots fifteen feet into the air. The ball reaches its highest point, and it seems to float for a moment. Suah spots the ball, and quickly positions himself underneath it.

Suddenly, everything seems to move in slow motion.

As the ball begins its descent, Suah flips into the air, his feet are above his head as he executes a textbook bicycle kick. His foot strikes the ball perfectly, and the ball rockets into the back of the net. Suah jumps to his feet and raises his arms briefly. Big celebrations are not his way.

The team mobs Suah. We embrace him.

He closes his eyes and a smile appears on his face. It's at that moment that I know that Suah is not thinking about scoring goals and winning games. He is thinking about his family.

Looking at Suah, I realize that he is something greater than I could ever be. He is beautiful, inside and out. But after meeting Suah and hearing his story, I know that I have learned from him. He has made me a better soccer player and more importantly, a better human being.

As for me, I have learned to face life on life's terms.

And as for Suah, as I watch him jog back to his position, I know that his new beginning has already begun.

⚽ **Questions on *Suah's Way*:**

1. Research the civil war in Liberia. How is Suah's situation different from other child soldiers in Liberia? What was the outcome of the war?

    _____

    _____

    _____

    _____

    _____

    _____

    _____

    _____

    _____

    _____

2. What are some of Suah's messages about healing and forgiveness? Give textual evidence to support your answer.

    _____

    _____

    _____

    _____

    _____

    _____

    _____

FOOTBALL: DOUBLE SESSIONS

"I found this sandbank by the Pearl River near my hometown, Columbia, Mississippi. I laid out a course of 65 yards or so. Sixty-five yards on sand is like 120 on turf. But running on sand helps you make your cuts at full speed. I try to pick the heat of the day to run in, but sometimes that sand will get so hot you can't stand in one place. It'll blister your feet. You get to the point where you have to keep pushing yourself. You stop, throw up and push yourself again. There's no one around to feel sorry for you."

—Walter Payton
(NFL Running Back)

Cancer. It touches everybody. Usually, it's a grandparent. Sometimes it's an aunt or uncle. Sometimes it's a friend. In some cases, it strikes closer to home, like a parent or maybe even a brother or sister. But what happens when the doctor looks down at you on the examination table and tells you, at the age of 17, that you have cancer?

I'll tell you what happens. Your entire body goes completely numb, and your brain freezes. It's as if you can't even have a coherent thought. Everything the doctor says after that sounds like "blah, blah, blah." All you can make out are the big words like Hodgkin's lymphoma, radiation, and chemotherapy. And you feel sick to your stomach because the people you knew that had cancer are now dead.

Besides, you are big and strong, and the starting linebacker on the Washington Massillon varsity football team. You are invincible, immortal. Cancer doesn't happen to people like you. It's the beginning of your senior year, the year you've been waiting for since the day you were old enough to play football.

You had the orange and black football in your crib on the day you were born. This is the year you've looked forward to since the day you saw your first varsity football game on Friday night under the lights, and you said to yourself, I am going to be the starting middle linebacker for the Massillon Tigers. You know the history. Your dad told you all about the legendary greatness of Chris Spielman.

Eventually, your emotions calm down and the numbness sets in.

After a while, the numbness wears off, and then you start to ask questions, and of course you pay attention to the big questions like: Is this kind of cancer treatable? Can it be beaten? How long does the treatment last? What is the survival rate? Because you have heard of people who have beaten cancer, you think that you can, too.

Quickly you become an expert at medical research on the Internet. Suddenly, all those research projects in school don't seem so ridiculous because you know where to look and what to look for. It's amazing how your thirst for knowledge goes off the charts when it's your life and your death. No longer do you surf Instagram and Twitter and check your text messages. Now, your server has the most hits on WebMd, because you need to know exactly what radiation and chemotherapy are, and what they are like, and how to deal with the side effects.

Double sessions for football practice start soon, but you won't be a part of them. Not this year. Your double sessions will be chemotherapy followed by radiation at the Cleveland Clinic's Taussig Cancer Center. The Sunday before treatment begins, your best friends are thinking about the next two grueling weeks of hard hits and soreness. Your dreaded anticipation is much different.

Your best friend Zach comes over on Sunday night. The problem is neither one of you knows what to say because the gravity of the situation is like nothing either of you has ever faced before. When he leaves, he gives you a hug and simply says, "Good luck,

David." Your best friend has never shown this much emotion. You know that Zach would do anything for you, just like you would do anything for him. You are like brothers.

The first day in the hospital is the beginning of the longest journey of your life. You check in at the registration desk, and wait with your parents because today is the day you start with the chemotherapy. You look around the waiting room: the big purple chairs and the simple wooden tables in front of them. The giant windows let in rays of sunlight, and the smell of bleach and cleaner fill the air. That hospital smell.

While you wait, you look out the window as cars drive by with people hurrying to work, and suddenly you realize how unimportant the things you used to worry about are, like your big social studies test, or who you were going to ask to the prom. Now, your worries run much deeper and the stakes are much higher. Doctors and nurses walk briskly past you in their pure white uniforms with nametags hanging from front pockets.

A nurse comes to get you with a wheelchair. "David Parker?" she asks.

You nod your head, but then say no to the use of the wheelchair, that you can walk just fine.

She responds, "There is a good chance you might not feel that way when the chemotherapy is over."

Reluctantly, you sit in the chair. Your dad offers to push, and you are glad that he is there, along with your mom and little sister. Dad wheels you down a long hallway into a room in the back of the building.

From your mom, you hear sniffles and swift inhales. She does her best to hide her tears.

Your sister trails behind and asks your mom, "Is David going to be okay?"

With confidence in her voice, your mom says, "Of course he is." But the look on her face tells another story.

In the room, there is a large window, and the sun is bright, giving warmth to the room. It's nine in the morning, and all you can think about is that your friends are starting football practice and the fact that you're not there. The very thing you live for has been taken from you.

Within minutes of getting settled in the room, a woman walks in carrying a quilt from an organization that supports patients with cancer.

She looks at you and says, "These blankets are handmade by cancer survivors." You can tell that she wants to cry and hug you because you are too young for this.

And then tears fill her eyes, and she hugs you, tightly. She hands you the blanket and whispers in your ear, "Fight the good fight."

You take the blanket from her and rest it on your lap and say, "Thank you."

"You're welcome," she says, as she rubs your back and forces a smile. She has two other blankets in her hand. "My work is not done for the day, but let me know if there is anything I can do." She hands you a card with her name and number on it.

Your dad gives her a handshake, and your mom gives her a hug. They both say, "Thank you" again and again. The kind lady waves as she heads out of your room.

When you really look at the blanket, you notice that it's covered with words and phrases like *Hope* and *Courage* and *Never Give Up* on it. A week ago a blanket like this would seem absurd, childish. But now you hold onto that blanket like it's gold, and the messages are the most important messages in the world. You know people who aren't fighters, people who have given up in the face of challenges. Or maybe they were fighters, but the cancer was just bigger.

But either way, you weren't brought up like that. You were taught to never give up under any circumstances, never give in. Football has given you that. Your coaches have taught you that no matter what the score, you give it your all until that final whistle blows. Coach always said, "It's your choice about whether or not you are willing to go the distance."

You decide to pretend that the months of treatment will be like your own personal football season… and you have to prepare just like you would for double sessions or any game on Friday night.

You have a new appreciation for your parents. Because up until a week ago, they embarrassed you because they cared so much about you, always wanted to know how things were going, asked how your day was at school. But now you know how lucky you are to have them in your life. And your annoying little sister suddenly becomes your best friend. You quickly find out she's not so immature and not nearly as clueless as you thought she was, because she has this devotion to you because you are her older brother, and she would do anything for you. And that makes tears well up in your eyes because you realize that you should have been a better big brother. You think about the fact that when she was always bothering you, you should have taken the time to listen to her, tell her that she's all right. You promise yourself that when this is all over, you will make a conscious effort to be a better big brother.

The nurse comes in and introduces herself. She slides on those blue medical hospital gloves. She doesn't have to poke around very much until she finds a vein, and then she swabs generously with the alcohol to clean the area. She explains what a PICC line is and how they will use it to give you the chemotherapy. She notices your muscles and comments on how strong you are. The nurse is friendly and pretty. She smiles a lot, and that helps. But it doesn't change the reality of the situation.

Because then come the bags of chemotherapy.

You have read so much about chemotherapy, how some people get sick. How some say it feels cold in their veins, and others say it's like a burning sensation. You have read that twenty years ago, just about everybody got sick from the treatment, but now they have anti-nausea medication and that helps to manage the side effects. So when the nurse offers you the anti-nausea medication, you say, "Yes" without hesitation. You figure it's better than throwing up in front of your family, even though they wouldn't mind. The nurse says it's going to take a while for the treatment.

It's then that your sister gives you a book that she checked out from the library because she thought it might help you. It's called *It's Not about the Bike.* You take the book from her and thank her.

When your family leaves for a minute to go get a snack from the vending machines and stretch their legs, you read Lance Armstrong's book like your life depends on it, because you think that it might have some answers as to how you're feeling and what you can do to get through this. Most of all, you want to identify with someone who understands how you feel. In the book, you find out that doctors gave him less than a fifty percent chance to live. And you decide that if he can beat cancer, so can you.

The weeks of treatment pass by slowly. Initially you decide to go to school during the first couple weeks of treatment, but that quickly changes when the fatigue sets in and the word gets out, and nobody looks at you like the star of the football team anymore.

Instead, you are this kid at school who has cancer. And even though the other students want to help you and offer to carry your books and help you in any way they can, you decide you will do your schoolwork at home and avoid the drama.

You manage to go to the first few football games, but you sit on the opposite side of the stadium and wear a hat to complete the disguise. Quickly, the games become painful to watch because this is your senior year, and you're supposed to be playing. The football team starts the first play of every game with only ten players on defense. This leaves a noticeable gap in the center of the field. Coach says it's so you know your place is waiting for you when you beat the cancer. You know this is a kind gesture, but it makes you feel like you're letting your team down even more. That's your position out there, and you are missing out on everything you have worked for since you played in your first organized football game. The pain you feel about not being on the field intensifies. This is not the way you pictured your senior year.

At the hospital, you see men and women who are older than you, and boys and girls that are much younger than you. You learn that cancer does not discriminate, and that there are many different kinds of cancer. And they all are scary and relentless. But you manage to make some new friends: a young girl who has bone marrow transplants and an older man who refuses to believe that he has cancer. She is fearless, unlike anyone you have ever met. She takes on the treatment with a fearless determination that says, "This thing ain't going to beat me." He explains that he is going to go on living until someone tells him differently. That cancer has nothing on him. You smile at that and admire his courage, and you decide that you will face your cancer in the same way.

You will not give it any respect.

After the first four weeks of chemotherapy, you are introduced to radiation therapy. The downstairs dungeon of radiation. The nurses are friendly, just to contrast with the radiation treatment, which is anything but. The radiation burns your skin, and gives you sores, but you take this on just like the chemotherapy.

Fatigue and nausea are a constant part of your life. Your once solid body is giving into the chemicals and the radiation. Six weeks into the treatment, your resiliency starts to fade. You look in the mirror and notice that your muscles have dwindled, and your linebacker-body isn't even close to what it was. And you start to wonder if all that "never giving up" is just a bunch of quotes that people make up just to give people hope.

So you start to think about death and God, and you pray like your life depends on it, because it does. You have reached the bottom rung of the ladder, the end of your rope. And you start to think about what's at the bottom of that rope, underneath or beyond. And you question if there's a vast eternity of nothingness. And that scares the hell out of you.

So you hope there's a God, a spirit, some place to go once you die. You think about the afterlife and eternity. The thoughts make you shiver. But you remember those Sunday mornings your parents made you get up for church, and you fought them tooth and nail. Now you're hoping that those frequent visits have given you some stock, some kind of spiritual investment, and you will be able to make some periodic withdrawals during this battle. And you think about that poster in the weight room that reads: When you get to the end of your rope, tie a knot... and hang on.

You think about overcoming the odds, like the story of David and Goliath. You see the cancer as the giant, but deep down you know you can win this battle. Something tells you that it's not your time. You still have lots of living to do.

And even though you have not been participating in your varsity football season, you have been recruited by big Division I schools like Ohio State, Michigan, and Penn State, because of an unbelievable junior year, so you tell yourself that you have a future that is worth fighting for. Football is an enormous part of it. As you look in the mirror, you see your body as it once was. You promise yourself that you will make it back. Be your old self once again.

You don't want to be seen by your friends, and you need a break from your family. Quickly, you find out that this process is a very lonely and daunting one. You don't want to inconvenience your friends; however, you don't want to be alone. You know they have football on their mind.

One day you get a visit from your friend, Zach. He is your best friend on the team, one of the other linebackers. You have been friends since the very first day of first grade. You hate having him see you this way. Tired, weak, and vulnerable. You reminisce about past football games, teachers you liked and didn't like, the senior prom, and graduation.

But then the conversation about football turns serious.

You say, "Football is getting me through this."

"But David, you've stopped coming to the games," Zach says.

You shake your head and try to explain. "No, the strength from running gassers and 40s. How coach would always say it's too easy to quit. It's too easy not to push yourself. Isn't it weird that's what's getting me through this?"

He shakes his head. "No," he agrees, "it makes all the sense in the world."

You smile at this because you always thought that your ideas didn't make sense. So you say, "That's what tells me I'm never going to give up. It's not in my blood. In the fourth quarter of the game, with two minutes left, and we're down by two touchdowns, I'm playing just as hard as the first snap. I've taken on the cancer in the same way."

Zach tells you how he remembers hearing a story about two brothers. One is sick and needs blood. The doctor tells the healthy brother that he has the same blood type, so he asks him if he will give his blood to help his sick brother. The healthy brother goes home and sleeps on it. He gets up the next day and tells his parents that he will do it. That he will give his blood. At the hospital, the doctor hooks him up to some IVs that begin to take his blood.

After a while, the healthy brother looks at the doctor and says, "When will I die?"

The doctor gets this confused look on his face and says, "You're not going to die. Why would you think that you're going to die?"

He says, "I'm giving my blood to my brother."

The doctor has to explain that he was just giving some of his blood, not all of it. That he would be just fine.

Zach looks at you with tears in his eyes, because you *are* the two brothers in the story.

He tells you that he would give you anything you need.

And you know he's telling the truth because you can see it in his eyes. It's the same look he's given you throughout your friendship and through the battles on the football field, where you have had each other's backs since Pee-wee football. Whenever you've needed him, he's been there. And you've been there for him.

The last four weeks of treatment are like the fourth quarter of a football game. You're tired, and some doubt creeps into your mind, and you question whether or not you have what it takes to finish the game, to win. But you know that you have never cheated in practice. You've run every single sprint to the best of your ability, never took a play off, never missed a practice. This has prepared you mentally. You know that you have put in the same effort with the treatment and that you can last this final four weeks and finish strong. Even though your body is broken down, your mind is still strong.

You go to the last few games of the football season, even though it tears you apart inside because even though you are in a fight for your very own life, you feel like you're letting your teammates down. You're supposed to be out on that field.

You make yourself get up each morning and walk. Even though you miss school and your friends, you know that if you beat the cancer, you will still have the second half of your senior year. You tell yourself that high school is just part of the journey and college will be a new start. You can be healthy. Even though cancer will always be a part of your life in some way, you want to put the helmet and shoulder pads on again and feel what it's like to be invincible.

The doctor comes to see you toward the end of your treatment. She uses words like remission and proper diet and tells you to keep an eye on things. She tells you that things look good, but there's always the chance that it could come back. There could be a recurrence. She tells you that, "You are not yet out of the woods."

After the conversation with the doctor, you think about your future. And four months ago, you had no idea what you wanted to do with your life other than play football. Now, you think about the possibility of becoming a doctor that helps children that are diagnosed with cancer. Because you were so afraid at the beginning of all this, you want to be the person that could make someone else's experience less scary.

You know now that your experience of having gone through chemotherapy and radiation could be a blessing for someone else. You can let them know what it's like, and you can tell them they can win this battle against cancer.

At the end of your treatment, on the way out of the hospital, you see the woman who gave you that blanket with all those words of encouragement, and you ask her, "What can I do to help pass out those blankets?"

She smiles real big and gives you a hug, tells you how to pass on the good will and make others feel like this journey is one that can be won, and more importantly that they are not alone. She leans over and whispers in your ear, "Fight the good fight."

And you know that the message is about more than cancer.

As you walk out of that hospital with your family after your final chemotherapy treatment, something inside you tells you that you will continue to fight this battle, not just for yourself, but for others as well.

On the drive home to Massillon, you pass a local high school near downtown Cleveland, and a football team is practicing outside. As the offense breaks the huddle, you can feel the adrenaline run through your veins, through your blood.

This feeling is the spark of life that you have lived on over the course of the treatment.

Football has given you that.

Your teammates have given you that.

Your family has given you that.

The doctors and nurses have given you that.

The other people you met in the hospital facing the same battle have given you that.

As you roll down your window and breathe in that crisp fall air, you know that deep down, no matter what life throws at you from here on out, you will never give up.

Looking at those football players out on that field, you think about wanting to be your old self.

But then you stop yourself because now you know, you can never be that person, nor do you want to be.

You will become something stronger.

And... something better.

🏈 Questions on *Double Sessions*:

1. Read the following passage from the short story. Answer the questions based on the passage:

   > At first, you don't want to be seen by your friends, but eventually, you need a break from your family. However, you don't want to be alone. Quickly, you find out that this process is a very lonely and DAUNTING one. But you don't want to inconvenience your friends. You know they have football on their mind.

   What does the word DAUNTING mean as it is used in the passage?

   a. hopeful
   b. overwhelming
   c. courageous
   d. fearless

2. How did you determine the meaning of the word DAUNTING? Explain what textual clues you used to help you determine the meaning of the word.

   _____

   _____

   _____

   _____

   _____

   _____

3. Most stories are written in either first or third person. This story is written in second person. Does this enhance the story or not? Why would the author choose second person to tell this particular story? How would the story be different if it were told in either first or third person?

_____

_____

_____

_____

_____

_____

_____

_____

_____

_____

_____

_____

_____

_____

_____

_____

_____

WINTER

BASKETBALL: IRON HORSE

"I believe with all my heart that athletics is one of the finest preparations for most of the intricacies and darknesses that human life can throw at us."

—Pat Conroy
(Author and Point Guard at the Citadel)

The train accelerates out of the turn, like LeBron James powering his way to the basket. As the black and yellow engine hits the straightaway, it stands tall. My best friend Joel and I squat down in the ditch along the side of the tracks as the connecting rods push and pull on the steel wheels of the train. As the train roars past us, the whistle lets out a loud scream. Deafening. It makes my ears ache. Despite all that, I love the size of the train, its sheer strength. The energy surges through my body. Most kids would throw rocks at it. Disrespect it. But not me. I respect everything about it. In fact, when I play basketball, I pretend I am the train. I become the train. Nothing can stop me. The problem is… it's the only time in my life I feel that way.

Once the train has passed, my buddy Joel taps me on the shoulder and says, "C'mon, Mike. Let's get out of here. Practice starts in ten minutes."

We walk on the snow-covered tracks toward Rockville High School, a small school south of Cincinnati, Ohio. These particular tracks are more than just train tracks. They serve as a wall, a barrier. They divide two towns and two ways of life.

"Big game tomorrow," Joel says, kicking at some rocks. His lanky, six foot two inch body slinks along next to me.

Nodding my head, I say, "Yeah, been thinkin' on it for a month now."

Joel smiles and says, "You gonna check Jimmy?"

"I imagine. I know his game better than anybody."

"You think you can hang with him, Mike?"

Shrugging my shoulders, I say, "I guess we'll find out."

As we continue our walk toward practice, I start thinking about how Jimmy used to live in Rockville. How his dad and my dad used to work for the city maintenance department. They used to drink together too, until my dad got laid off and his dad hit the lotto. I'm not even kidding. His dad hit the Ohio $5,000 a week for life lotto. Within a month, they moved across the tracks, right into Kingston. Up until then, Jimmy and I were best friends. Played hoops together every day after school. Since he left, we've drifted farther and farther apart. Even though I would never tell Joel, I miss Jimmy more than I would a brother. Our one-on-one games in Jimmy's driveway are legendary. Black eyes and bloody noses have resulted from those games. Despite the violence associated with those games, they are the source of our friendship. They are also the source of our desire to win. Those games have made us the players we are today: aggressive and fearless. Plus, I can't think of two guys that love the game as much as we do.

Joel's breath shoots up into the cold winter air, and he says, "You know Jimmy's gonna be first team All-state. He's been rewriting the record books. Had thirty points the other night. North Carolina and Duke both want him."

Nodding my head, I say, "Yeah, he's had a great year. There's no doubt about that." Thinking about my driveway match-ups with Jimmy, and my occasional victory over him, my confidence begins to grow. Looking at Joel, I say, "I'm gonna shut him down."

"No doubt," says Joel, as he picks up a piece of gravel and pitches it into the woods. When we get to the corner drugstore, Joel stands as the lookout. I case the store, looking for the owner, Mr. Bishop. His back is turned, stocking Marlboros behind the counter. Slipping into the back of the store, I steal a pair of sunglasses off the rack and slide them into my pocket. At the back of the store, I open the door to the beer and soda. I grab a pint of whiskey and a Pepsi and slide the whiskey into the front of my pants and pull my shirt over it. At the register, I give Mr. Bishop three dollars for the Pepsi and a pack of Trident I pull off the rack.

After walking out of the store, Joel and I disappear behind the building and twist the cap off the whiskey. Joel takes a swig and smiles. I grab onto it like it's my life source, drinking it down, but it's not enough. It won't take the edge off.

Joel thinks the drink is for fun, just screwin' around. Not me. I need it.

The panic attacks that I get have the ability to consume me, shoot through my entire body and paralyze me. Immobilize me. It's gotten to the point where I've given the panic a name. I call it the Beast.

Sometimes, the Beast lasts ten minutes; sometimes, it's an hour. On some days, a dull version of the Beast can last all day. The only time I can escape the Beast are those few moments when that train rumbles by or when I'm on the basketball court. When I need to, I use alcohol or pills. It's the only way I know how to deal.

Putting on the sunglasses, I chew the gum on the way to basketball practice, thinking it will cover up the smell of the alcohol. And then, out of nowhere, the Beast pays me a visit. I can feel it coming on, but there's nothing I can do to stop it. The Beast starts in my mind... and then spreads to my shoulders, and slides down my spine. Everything tingles. Complete fear. I want to cry, but I don't want to embarrass myself in front of Joel. He knows about the Beast, but he doesn't understand, can't relate.

This is *my* personal hell.

Each day seems harder than the next. The doctor says it's depression, but I don't feel sad… just lost, and afraid, afraid that the Beast will never leave me alone.

When we get to the gym, I slide off my warm-ups and lace up my high tops. In the gym, the Beast temporarily subsides, gives me a moment of solace. A few of the guys are already there, shooting jumpers and foul shots. We only have six guys on the Rockville High School team, just enough to scrimmage three on three. Joel is the only Jewish kid that lives in Rockville, and my buddy Danny, who is all of five eight, brags about how his great grandfather came right off the boat from Ireland. Standing at six foot three inches tall, Trevan is one of three black kids that live on our side of the tracks. Juan is six feet tall and the only Hispanic in Rockville. Luke is our six foot five inch center, and his father is the minister at our church. Swear to God.

Our coach is old man Porter, the school's janitor. He's so old that we think that one day he's going to just shrivel up or simply turn to dust.

When you're really playing well, and shooting the lights out, he'll say things like, "You're hotter than cow dung on a hot shingle." No one is sure if this is bad or good, so we just look at each other and laugh.

Porter is a student of the game, and he has made us share his passion. He tells us to watch YouTube videos of Magic Johnson and Isaiah Thomas. We watch Dr. J dunk from the foul line, Michael Jordan lean into a jam, like Superman, and Larry Bird stroke threes on the parquet floor in the Boston Garden. Shoot, he even made us read up on James Naismith, the dude who invented the game. He says that if we want to play the game, we have to respect it and know where it came from. I can appreciate and understand that. Basketball is the one thing I love.

We pick up teams. It's Joel, Trevan, and me against Danny, Juan, and Luke. Porter blows his whistle. "Listen up, boys," he says, clearing his throat from the second pack of cigarettes he's smoked already today. "We got them boys from the other side of the tracks tomorrow night. They've been a thorn in my side… a pain in my… You know what I mean. I wanna beat those guys more than you'll ever know."

Thing is, we do know. The rivalry between Rockville and Kingston is older than us. The people in Kingston drive the fancy cars, have the nicer houses, and go to the newer schools.

We have the train tracks. We have the run down houses. And each other.

Porter runs his fingers through his long grey hair, spits his chewing tobacco into an empty Coke can, and shouts, "Let's go! Run it!"

Joel zips the pass out to me on the wing. As soon as the ball hits my hands, I go to another place. It's quiet, serene, completely away from the Beast. Danny digs in, with one arm up and one down. He's giving me the baseline. Dribbling to my left, I quickly cross over and drive hard to the basket. Juan helps out on D, but that leaves Trevan wide open.

I deliver a crisp, no-look, bounce pass right on the money. Trevan's dreadlocks fly out to the side as he lays the ball in the hoop with a soft finger roll.

Porter shouts, "That's what I'm talking about! Good look, Mike! Good look! Way to dish it! Way to dish it! You're hotter than bird poop on asphalt! Steve Nash couldn't have delivered it better!" Porter blows his whistle. "Run it again!"

We run the plays, our motion offense against a stout man-to-man defense. I deliver behind-the-back passes to crisp backdoor cuts. When I'm on the court, my mind is clear, and the fear melts away. For a short time, I feel alive.

Trudging home in the sullen slush of late winter, I look up into the blue-black sky. On the tracks, there is a constant shaking under my feet. The five o'clock train is coming. Moving off to the side, I stand in the woods, leaning up against a tree. The iron horse thunders past me, and the vibrations bounce through my body. I admire its strength. Pretend I am it. Strong. Fearless. There will be another one along at nine. It's the only thing in my life that I have come to count on.

Home. Collapsing front porch and drooping shutters. Mom passed out on the couch. After pouring myself some vodka from her bottle, I cover her with a blanket and kiss her on the forehead.

In my room, I dig out the pills from the back of my sock drawer, and take a couple. As I sit in bed, my thoughts shift to my neighbor and the abuse. I curse myself for letting it happen. He was older, and I wanted him to like me. Maybe it was because my dad was never around. In my head, I put myself back in my neighbor's house, but this time I pretend that I am older and can protect my younger self. In my mind, I punish him for the things that he did...

Staring at my Kevin Durant poster and then at the long crack in the plaster on my wall, I think about death, because the alternative of facing life on a daily basis with the Beast is unbearable. It's that bad. I wonder what death is like. Is it that bright white light that you hear about in books and in the movies? That image creates a feeling of peace, and for a moment, I breathe easy. In my mind, I try to imagine my own funeral. The guys from the team would be there, my mom, maybe my dad if he's sober. Imagining the lid of the casket closing on top of me makes me shiver, and I am brought back to reality. A reality that, unfortunately, I have not yet figured out how to escape.

Anticipating our game tomorrow night against Kingston, and forgetting about my life for a while, I toss and turn in my bed, until eventually... I fall asleep.

The next morning, after a hot shower, I get dressed and make my way to school. Classes remind me that school is a waste of time. I don't pay attention to anything, except for my math teacher who has long blonde hair, blue eyes, and is right out of college. I'm not sure what love is, but I'm pretty sure I'm in love with her. At lunch, because the Beast is lurking, I sneak out behind the school and take two more pills. And for the time being, I hold the Beast at bay.

During sixth and seventh period, the anxiety climbs like King Kong on the Empire State Building. Somehow, I manage to make it through science and social studies, but by eighth period English, the Beast has completely taken over my body. It relentlessly pulsates through me, making me want to run and hide. My body goes numb, and then, I am completely paralyzed.

In eighth period English, my teacher, Mr. Gradishaw, explains how we are going to learn about Greek mythology.

Despite the overwhelming presence of the Beast, I try to focus on the story he reads out loud to the class called: "Pandora's Box." It's all about how Pandora and her husband Epimetheus get a dowry from the Gods, and part of the dowry is this little wooden box. In the story, they call it a casket.

Images of my own funeral and my casket flash through my mind.

Epimetheus tells Pandora not to open the box, but because Hera gives Pandora the gift of curiosity, she eventually can't help herself. She opens it, and out comes disease, sorrow, spite, malice, and all the disasters of the world.

While I listen to Mr. Gradishaw explain all this, I wonder where anxiety fits into all of those disasters and how it has focused itself on me.

Gradishaw interrupts my thoughts when he says it's like the Bible's story of Adam and Eve. He explains that Pandora is inconsolable because of what she's done, but Epimetheus suggests that there might be something left in the box. Pandora opens it again, and Epimetheus is right. Out floats a fragile little thing with wings.

"Look, it is Hope," Pandora explains. "Even though it is fragile, it will always be there for us."

Toward the end of class, Mr. Gradishaw explains that he is finishing up his counseling degree to help students deal with all the sorrows of the world. He mentions that after teaching English for twenty years, he has been called to help students in a different way. For a moment, I can't help but wonder if Mr. Gradishaw could help me.

The bell rings to end the period, and I make my way out of the building. On the way home from school, two things swirl in my brain: tonight's basketball game against Jimmy and Pandora's box. Walking on the tracks, I wonder what the hell I did to deserve the wrath of sorrow and anxiety from that box.

The Kingston gym is like New York's Madison Square Garden compared to the hole-in-the wall where we play in Rockville. Jimmy Jackson and his boys from Kingston warm up in their fire-engine-red uniforms. They all wear the new LeBron James Nike shoes. Rumor has it, Jimmy's dad bought them for the team. They are the Chicago Bulls, and Jimmy is their Michael Jordan. Jimmy has more game than just about anybody in the state. He's six foot three with mad skills. I'm only five ten on a good day, but I want nothing more than to prove to everybody, most importantly myself, that I am not worthless.

Porter tells me to stay on Jimmy like stink on scat. He grunts and then coughs, slapping me on the butt.

During the warm-ups, Jimmy comes up to me and says, "What's up, Mike?"

We shake hands and lean in for a half hug. "Been waiting for this game all season," I say.

"I'm going to own you tonight," he says with his typical swagger.

"We'll see," I say, feeling the adrenaline shoot through my body.

During warm-ups, my anxiety grows. But strangely, during the last two minutes before the game starts, my anxiety melts away.

In the huddle before the game, Porter's words are drowned out by my thoughts about Jimmy. I know that even though he now lives in Kingston, he's no different than me. The money has gotten them a bigger house, but not a better life. Jimmy hasn't had it easy at Kingston. He still has to deal with his "situation." Even though he's the star of the team, some of the kids there make fun of him because he is a mixed race. His mom is half black and half Native American, and his dad, who is white, is no different than mine, a drunk. Even though Jimmy is the star of the Kingston team, he is not considered one of them. I've heard that the students make fun of him behind his back. Cowards.

Referees blow their whistles, and the game is on. After getting the tip from Danny, we run our motion offense. Jimmy goes for the steal, but I dribble behind my back into a collapsing defense and dish a no-look pass to a hard-cutting Joel, who lays it off the glass, soft, like a hummingbird with tired feet. Jogging back down the court, Jimmy delivers a stiff elbow to my shoulder. I absorb the blow.

Jimmy plays the point. Directing traffic. He dribbles low and posts me up on the block, using his height. When he backs into me, I slide to the side, and he falls into the key. Swiping the ball, I drive down the court and cut into the lane. Drawing contact from their other guard, I lay it off the glass for two points and the foul. Stepping to the foul line, I complete the three-point play.

Half way into the first quarter, our fast start stalls, and Jimmy Jackson shows why he is All-State, with smooth takes to the basket, crisp no-look passes, and a baseline-dunk for good measure. Jimmy is way better than I remember from our driveway battles. He has refined his game.

At the end of the first quarter, we are down 15 to 10. In the huddle, Porter says, "You boys are playing your hearts out. You're in the game. We're going to pull out of the man-to-man defense and put a box-in-one on Jimmy. Everybody plays zone." Then he points at me and says, "Except you, Mike. You're man-to-man on Jimmy. You gotta shut him down. He's their guy. Everything runs through him. Deny him the ball." Porter gets this big grin on his face, and with fire in his eyes, he shouts above the cheers from the crowd, "Can you do that, Mike?"

"Yes, sir," I say. My heart believes I can shut him down, just like I told Joel, but when I look at the Kingston bench and see Jimmy, the doubt in me is strong.

The buzzer shakes me out of my thoughts.

"Let's go. Hands in," says Porter. "Rockville on three. One, two, three…"

In unison, we all shout, "ROCKVILLE!"

The box-in-one defense against Jimmy works, and I manage to hold him to only two baskets in the second quarter. But their big men dominate the boards and get easy put-back points off missed shots. We manage to score on a few breakaway lay-ups and outside jump shots, but as the second quarter winds down, it is clear we need a new strategy.

When the buzzer goes off at halftime, we are down ten: 32 to 22.

In the locker room, Porter tries to energize us. He explains to us how we need to push through the fatigue. Push through the self-doubt. He grits his teeth and tells us we are sick dog warriors, and that we would rather die than go down without a fight. And to the five other guys in the room, this seems extreme, but to me, it makes all the sense in the world. I've got nothing to lose. I would die to win this game, for this game. I put every part of me into this game. With six months until we start our next season, and the power of the Beast, I don't know if I'll make it.

We come out like crazed dogs in the third quarter. But Kingston comes out just as strong, matching us lay-up for lay-up, and jump shot for jump shot. Jimmy's aggressiveness matches my relentless defense. Our match-up is not unlike one of our classic drive-way battles.

Despite our team's hustle, diving for loose balls, and white-on-rice defense, Kingston increases their lead to seventeen by the end of the third quarter. The scoreboard reads: Kingston 50 Rockville 33.

In between periods, Porter waves us over to the bench and shouts above the roar of the crowd, "Have you boys had enough? Is this how you want your season to end?"

"No, sir," we all say in unison.

"Is this good enough for you?" he asks again, this time with more intensity.

"NO, SIR!" we all shout.

"All right, listen up. This quarter, we're going to a full court press. We are everywhere at once, like dogs on a hunt." The spit flies from Porter's mouth. "IS THAT CLEAR?" he shouts above the chants from the crowd. "Let's go, hands in. TEAM on three... One, two, three..."

"TEAM!"

The buzzer sounds, and with a new sense of resolve, we head back onto the court.

At the beginning of the fourth quarter, we slap on our full court press. We dig in, and I get two quick steals and two lay-ups, to make the score 50 to 37. Our constant pressure causes the Kingston Knights to begin to fumble the ball and miss open looks.

After intercepting a pass on the press from Jimmy, I pull up for a three, catching nothing but net, making it a ten-point game. We are on fire, and the Knights have gone cold.

And as old man Porter would say, "We are hotter than dung on a tin roof." Our press takes their big men out of the game, and they don't have any other good ball handlers besides Jimmy. After two more steals, Danny and Luke hit back-to-back jumpers to pull within six points.

Kingston calls a timeout, and we hustle over to our bench. With four minutes left in the fourth quarter, the score is now: Kingston 50 Rockville 44.

The momentum has shifted.

Porter growls, "You boys are right back in it! The press is killing 'em! Keep up the pressure! It's your game to win! Don't let it slip away!" Porter pauses and looks each one of us in the eye. "Anybody have anything else?"

With hands on knees, and sweat running down Luke's face, he says, "Fellas, I've been praying all week about this game. I've been talking to my dad about it. God is on our side."

Despite the intensity of the moment, we all smile at this.

However, after we break the huddle, and within ten seconds after the game resumes, Jimmy gets the ball and elevates after beating me on a backdoor cut. I look up in amazement as Jimmy seems to jump a second time while he is in the air, the muscles in his legs flexing, urging him up toward the heavens. He power dunks the ball with two hands, rattling the backboard, and then he hangs from the rim.

The dunk is nothing short of divine. And for a moment, I think about what Luke said about God being on our side, and I think that maybe, just maybe, God... is on Jimmy Jackson's side.

While Jimmy runs along the sideline and pumps his fists and celebrates his dunk with the crowd, I get the inbounds pass from Trevan and push the ball up the floor and draw contact in the lane. I let a teardrop runner go that hits nothing but net, for two points and a foul shot. After I make the foul shot, the score is 47 to 52 with three minutes to go.

Porter calls time out. We huddle around him. "Keep up the pressure. They're having trouble getting the ball up the court. Full court press, like your life depends on it!" he shouts. Porter's entire body is shaking.

Even though we are down five, we know it's our game to win.

We lock down on the full court press and get a ten second call and a turnover. I inbound the ball to Joel who comes off a high screen from Luke and hits a three to make it a two-point game with 1:45 to play.

Kingston brings the ball up the court, and their forward throws a weak pass to Jimmy cutting toward center court. I steal the pass at half court. Then, I dribble around two defenders and drive the lane like the powerful iron horse.

Their six foot eight inch center stands in the key, waiting for me, but I pull up on a dime, shooting a jumper that ties the game, 52 to 52, with one minute to play.

With a look of pure determination on his face, Jimmy brings the ball up the court for Kingston.

I slide my feet, making Jimmy change direction up and down the floor.

He raises two fingers, calling out a play to his teammates.

While guarding Jimmy, I think about the train tracks, all of our one-on-one battles in the driveway, and I dig in deeper, want it more. Jimmy drives hard to his left, but I anticipate the move and steal the ball. I head down the court and drive toward the basket. Everything goes quiet. It's just me, the ball, and a fast-closing Jimmy Jackson. Because he's not going to give me the bunny, he fouls me hard, and we go crashing into the mat on the wall behind the basket.

Immediately, I jump to my feet and give Jimmy a hard shove. He pushes me back, and we are chest-to-chest, talking smack.

"Too tough for you!" I shout at Jimmy, pointing my finger at him. "This is our game."

Jimmy shakes his head, waves a finger at me, and says, "Not tonight, Mike. Not tonight."

Neither one of us backs down. Our teammates sprint over, and the mob of players begins pushing and shoving under the basket. Neither team gives any ground. The roar from the crowd urges both sides on. They want blood.

The referees blow hard on their whistles and try to jump in between the pack of players. The Kingston coaches and Coach Porter pull players out of the mob and somehow manage to separate the two teams.

Once the referees get everything sorted out, they warn both teams, and threaten to kick out the next player who starts anything.

Stepping to the foul line, I stroke the first free throw, swish. The second shot hits the front of the rim, rolls around, and falls off the side of the cylinder.

Their center grabs the rebound and hands the ball to Jimmy. Jimmy motions for everyone to clear out, so he can bring the ball up the floor. I check him as the seconds on the clock wind down.

We are up one, with twenty seconds left in the game.

Tonight is our night.

This is our time.

Ten seconds on the clock.

Turning him up and down the court, Jimmy crosses over and beats me to the basket.

With five seconds on the clock, he drives down the center of the lane.

Joel drops off his man to help out on Jimmy.

Jimmy passes the ball to his teammate, and Danny rotates to help out Joel, but that leaves Danny's man wide open and cutting to the basket.

Two seconds on the clock.

Desperately, I try to rotate back to Danny's man, but the Kingston forward gets the pass and lays it in off the glass as the clock expires. The ball slides through the net.

We lose… 54 to 53.

The Kingston fans go crazy, stomping their feet on the bleachers. Dropping to my knees underneath the basket, I bury my face in my hands, unwilling to accept the loss. From the cheering of the Kingston fans, I can actually feel the gym rocking underneath me. They have won… again.

Joel comes over and helps me to my feet. "You all right, Mike?"

"Yeah, yeah, I'm okay." I glance over and see the satisfied look on Jimmy's face.

In the locker room after the game, Porter, with moist eyes, huddles us up and says, "I love you boys as if you were my own sons. You all played like warriors tonight. It was one of the greatest games I've ever been a part of. Keep your heads up. You've got nothin' to be ashamed of." He lets out a deep breath and says, "Life will go on. Tomorrow is a new day."

After we get dressed, we leave the locker room. Jimmy is standing outside the door waiting for me. He comes up to me and says, "Hey, Mike. Good game tonight."

"You, too," I say.

Jimmy smiles and says, "You were the best player on the floor tonight."

"You played a hell of a game," I say.

He waves me off. "It's about more than the game. I miss hanging out," Jimmy says.

"Yeah, me too."

Jimmy says, "My old man got a hoop for our driveway. The weather is supposed to warm up this week. You want to come by the house?"

I nod my head. "Sounds good. I'll give you a call this week."

As I head out into the parking lot, I tell Joel and his mom that I'm going to walk home. The night air is crisp, clear. "The fresh air will do me good," I tell them.

Walking on the train tracks at 8:58, I replay the game in my head. How I should have anticipated Jimmy's drive. How I should have stood my ground. How I let us down. How I let down Porter. The Beast creeps in. The fear fills me up. On the tracks, I think about death again, imagine my funeral in my head, all my friends gathered around.

How could I put that pain on them? How could I put that pain on my mom? It would be the most selfish act in the world. But I wouldn't have to face the day and the thoughts of my neighbor. I wouldn't have to face the Beast. And that... gives me a sense of peace.

The tracks vibrate. The nine o'clock is right on time. It accelerates down the straightaway like Jimmy Jackson on his way to the basket. The tears fill my eyes as I remain on the tracks. The whistle blows fierce. The train is about four hundred yards away and moving fast.

Thirty seconds on the clock.

At two hundred yards, I can begin to feel its power. The iron horse closes in, and the Beast in me roars. My feet stand firmly on the tracks.

Fifteen seconds on the clock.

The whistle thunders, urging me to get out of the way. The train closes in.

Closer.

Ten seconds on the clock.

This time... I stand my ground.

Five seconds on the clock. Four, three, two...

Just as the train is about to strike, I leap from the tracks and roll down the five-foot hill to safety.

Looking up from the bed of gravel, the iron horse rumbles past me with all its might, and the ground shakes beneath me. I let out a deep breath, and all I can hear is the rumble, rumble, rumble of the train on the tracks.

It takes me a minute to collect myself. My mind spins, and my heart pounds in my chest. After rising to my feet, I steady myself.

Wiping the tears from my face, I think about what to do. I can't hold a thought. Everything is confusing and distant.

As I walk toward my house, Porter's words pop in my head... "Push through the self-doubt. Tomorrow is a new day."

Looking up into the clear night sky and the stars above, I have a new vision, and for some reason, on this night, the vision has never been clearer. It's about living the best way I know how despite the darkness.

Despite the fear of the Beast.

And my new vision is about hope and how fragile, and ... how powerful, it is. This makes me think about what Mr. Gradishaw said about him becoming a counselor, and I think that maybe he can help. Because I know how hard it is to make it on my own, I consider seeing him first thing Monday morning.

And then, I think about playing Jimmy Jackson in his driveway on his new hoop.

Tomorrow.

Questions on *Iron Horse*:

1. What is the meaning of the word DEAFENING in the following passage from the short story: "As the train roars past us, the whistle lets out a loud scream. DEAFENING. It makes my ears ache. Despite all that, I love the size of the train, its sheer strength. The energy surges through my body."

   a. Something that is bothersome
   b. Something one cannot hear
   c. Something that is very loud
   d. Something that is distracting

1a. Which words did you use to determine the meaning of the word DEAFENING?

   a. the whistle lets out a loud scream
   b. it makes my ears ache
   c. I love the size of the train
   d. Both A and B

2. What is the meaning of the word SERENE in the following passage from the short story: "Joel zips the pass out to me on the wing. As soon as the ball hits my hands, I go to another place. It's quiet, SERENE, completely away from the Beast. Danny digs in, with one arm up and one down. He's giving me the baseline."

   a. Angry
   b. Anxious
   c. Peaceful
   d. Upsetting

2a. What context clues did you use to determine the meaning of the word SERENE?

_____

_____

_____

3. Kingston and Rockville are the two main settings in the short story. How does the name of each town represent the town in some way? How do the two very different settings play an important role in the story?

_____

_____

_____

_____

4. Symbolism in a story is when something represents more than what it is. What does the train symbolize in this story?

_____

_____

4a. Use textual evidence to support this idea:

_____

_____

_____

WRESTLING: HEART OF A CHAMPION

"Gold medals aren't really made of gold. They're made of sweat, determination, and a hard-to-find alloy called guts."

—Dan Gable
(Olympic Wrestling Champion)

Ohio has some of the best high school wrestling in the country, and today, I have the opportunity to interview one of the toughest, most feared, two-time state champions, Woody Fletcher. Woody and I sit at a table in the back room of a local restaurant after ordering their famous barbeque and spicy garlic chicken wings. The room is filled with about ten booths lining the walls of the place and twelve or so tables in the middle. Each table or booth is filled with customers for their Tuesday night fifty-cent wing special. There is a general hum of conversation around the room. Looking at my notepad, I scan my list of questions. I have been anticipating my interview with Woody for a long time. This interview will be the cover story for our final edition of the school newspaper.

Looking up at Woody from my notepad, I ask, "So, how's it going?"

Woody's intense, icy-blue eyes seemingly look through me. And then he softens, a little bit. "Good, George. How are you?" he asks, sipping his iced tea.

"Okay," I say, shifting uncomfortably in my chair, "thanks for meeting me for the interview." I jot down *Woody Fletcher* in my notebook, put a rectangle around his name, and then circle it.

"No problem," says Woody. He takes off his sweatshirt. He is wearing a blue T-shirt with gold letters that reads: UNIONVILLE WRESTLING: ONLY THE STRONG SURVIVE. The shirt has cut-off sleeves that expose his tattoos that wind and twist up his forearms and over his well-defined biceps. His tattoos are made up of faces and eyes and fingers. It's hard to make sense of the design. A bar is pierced through his left eyebrow. Woody is all of five foot six inches tall, and he has died his Mohawk an almost florescent blonde color. Even though his Mohawk would light the way,

Woody Fletcher is the last person I would want to meet in a dark alley.

I, on the other hand, am George Miller, the senior editor of the Unionville High School newspaper. At six feet two inches tall, lanky and awkward are words that even I would use to describe me.

Woody and I are as different as oil and water, but we grew up together, went to grade school together. To some degree, we are friends, acquaintances at least.

"So, should we just get started?" I ask.

"Fire away," he says.

Looking down at my list of questions, I ask, "When did you know that you wanted to wrestle?"

Woody scoots his chair up closer to the table. Taps his thumbs on the table as he considers the question, and then says, "My brother won a state championship for Unionville as a senior. I remember sitting in the packed arena with the crowd cheering like crazy. I wasn't even wrestling, but I had this adrenaline rush that made me feel like I could take on the world, and win. I remember thinking to myself, *I'm going to be a state champion some day*. If I had that adrenaline rush just watching my brother, I could only imagine what it would be like to actually be on the mat, winning a state championship. I was only a freshman at the time, but I knew I could do it."

Scribbling down his response, I ask another question. "This year you won your second state championship. Was this year's championship sweeter than the first one?"

Woody bobs his head back and forth. Maybe he's contemplating the question, or maybe, it's because it seems as if he is in constant motion. "Last year was unexpected. I was the underdog. No one thought I could do it. I wasn't even seeded. Winning that first state title as an underdog was awesome, but it was only an individual title. This year, we won a team title. It was the first one in the history of our school." A wide smile shows his pride in this accomplishment. "That made it much more meaningful to me."

I give Woody the double thumbs up and say, "I saw the signs they put on each corner of the city."

Woody nods his head and says, "Pretty cool, huh?"

"Very cool." After writing down Woody's answer about being more proud of the team title, I ask, "Why the Mohawk?"

Woody rubs the top of his head and runs his fingertips through his hair, and then he says, "There's a history there. The Iroquois Indians wore them into battle to intimidate their enemy. The only difference was their hair was plucked out. Not shaved. United States soldiers in World War II had Mohawks to intimidate the Germans. Mostly paratroopers." Woody rubs his hands together and then he cracks his knuckles. Looking at me, he says, "It gives me an advantage on the mat. Anything that I can do to make myself harder to beat… the better. I'll take any advantage I can get."

In my notebook, I write down MOHAWK in capital letters, and I wonder how Woody Fletcher knows so much about the Iroquois, World War II paratroopers, and Mohawks. When I finish jotting down the notes, I ask, "Where did you get the drive to be a state champion?"

Folding his arms and leaning forward on the table, he says, "My brothers. We were always wrestling. They were always pushing me to get better, to be the best." He laughs to himself for a second and then continues. "They never let me win, and that made me want to win in the worst way. I hated losing to them." He pauses for a moment, unfolds his arms, and then points down at my notebook and says, "Wait a minute. Erase that. Put my mom. Write that down. She's the rock of our family. She's my inspiration. She's overcome a lot in her life."

I put a single line through Woody's "~~brothers~~" answer and write down: MOM.

Leaning back from the table, he rubs his hands together and closes his eyes, like the question is really making him think, and he wants to give just the right answer. After a long exhale, he says, "You know, the more I think about it... truth is... it's my dad."

"Your dad?" I ask, putting question marks by MOM?? And then, I underline <u>MY DAD!</u> with an exclamation point next to it.

"Yeah, even though he hasn't been around much, he's still had a huge impact on my life. My parents got divorced when I was in second grade. Pretty much tore our family apart." Woody is quiet for a moment, and then he says, "He's a leading veterinarian in the state."

"I didn't know that," I say.

Woody nods his head. "Yeah, he works mostly with horses. If anybody has a problem with their horse, they go to my dad. He has worked with some of the best racehorses in the country. My dad didn't want to be a good vet. He wanted to be the best. Even though we're not very close, that's probably the most important thing I've taken from my dad. If you're going to do something, don't do it half-assed. Be the best."

"So, your dad works with horses?" I ask, putting a rectangle around the word horses and then add a question mark and then an exclamation point.

```
┌─────────────┐
│  HORSES?!   │
└─────────────┘
```

Woody taps his fingers on the table, gets this serious look on his face, and says, "Did you know that Secretariat won the Triple Crown? He won the Kentucky Derby, then Belmont, and he finished by winning the Preakness Stakes at Pimlico."

In my notebook, I write down Secretariat? with a question mark next to the name. I look up at Woody and say, "I don't know much about horseracing. It sounds like you're passionate about it. How do you know so much about racehorses?"

"It's really the only connection I have with my dad." He pauses for a moment and then says, "Did you know that Secretariat had a heart that was two times bigger than the hearts of the other racehorses? All anyone could do was admire the engine. Secretariat won all those races because his heart was bigger."

I look at Woody in disbelief. Mohawks and tattoos don't talk about such things, much less bars in eyebrows. "Is there a connection there?"

"Where?"

"With Secretariat?"

Woody takes another sip of iced tea and nods his head. "When you're a state champion, the expectations are higher. People don't see you as human. You're like a thoroughbred, and a means to an end. Coaches and teammates want you because you're a winner, and you can make the city a winner. It becomes very impersonal. You start to feel less human and more like a machine. Made for the purpose of winning."

When the wings are delivered to the table, we dig in. The smell of my garlic wings and Woody's barbeque wings fills my nose. As I watch Woody eat, these thoughts run through my head. I never would have thought Woody Fletcher had this kind of depth. His outward persona was stud, athlete, jock, and that was it. Never in a million years could I imagine there was more to Woody Fletcher than being a high school wrestler. Because I didn't anticipate these kinds of answers coming from him, I want to know more.

"Besides your family, what other influences did you have?"

"Nobody becomes a state champion alone. I had great coaches. Coach D was like a father to me. He taught me the technical part of the sport. My brothers made me more physical, but Coach D made me a tactician. I could take my opponent apart on technicalities. It got to the point where I could wrestle either with brute force or purely on technique."

"Did you ever wrestle coach D in practice? I understand he was a collegiate All American."

"I have in the past, but this year he brought in a guy right out of college to help coach the team. His name is Frank Sharpe. Frank is about my size and height, and he was an NCAA champion. We drilled every day in practice. He made me better. After wrestling an NCAA champion during the week, the high school matches seemed easy."

"Other than that, did you train differently?"

"My last period of the day was a free period. I ran everyday with Jeff Davis."

"Doesn't Jeff run cross country and track?" I ask.

Woody swallows a bite of his chicken wing, clears his throat and says, "Yeah, Jeff runs track and cross country. He would push me on our run, and then I would run with the team during practice, and then I hit the weight room three times a week." Woody washes down his wings with some iced tea.

"What made you do so much extra work?" I ask.

"You know, it's funny. I was told something a while ago, but I remember it like it was yesterday. Our 8th grade football coach always told us that our competition is always working, always trying to get better, and one day we're going to meet that competition. And it's going to boil down to who has been working harder. He told us that there is really no secret to success. The answer is simple: Hard work. If you want to win, you have to put in the time. If you want to be the best, you have to go above and beyond what the other guy is doing. You have to be willing to make all the necessary sacrifices."

I copy down Woody's answer into my notebook: *Make the necessary sacrifices. Go above and beyond what the other guy is doing.*

Woody pauses for a moment and then says, "That, and I'm afraid to slip. I'm afraid to fail. That fear of losing motivates me. I promised myself I would never lose because I was outworked. Never." Woody bites into a wing and chews.

I copy down this additional information: *The fear of losing motivates me. I'm afraid to fail. I promised myself to never lose because I was outworked! NEVER!*

"So, you were afraid of failing?" I ask, wondering how someone with seemingly so much confidence could be afraid of anything.

Woody shifts uncomfortably in his chair, like this question has caused some discomfort, exposed some vulnerability. "Well, yeah, who isn't afraid of failing, in front of your friends, your family, in front of an entire town?"

Nodding my head, I say, "I get it. So what do you think prevented you from failing?"

"I might not have always been the better wrestler, but I was always in better shape than my opponents, had better endurance. Because I spent so much time in the weight room, I was stronger. Because I worked harder than my opponents, I never got tired. I felt like I could outlast anyone on the mat. And I did."

Writing down Woody's answer, I motion toward his plate and say, "You sure did order a lot of food."

He smiles. "I'm on a strict diet for five months out of the year for wrestling. It's time to eat."

Moving down my list of questions, I ask, "Is wrestling your favorite sport?"

Woody laughs. "Actually, from the bottom to the top. Wrestling is my least favorite."

"Seriously?" From a two-time state champion, I didn't expect this answer.

"Yeah, then comes track. I run the 300 IM hurdles, long jump, and run the 4 X100 and 4 X 400 relays. My favorite events in track are the relays. It's the closest the sport comes to being a team sport. I like team sports." Woody gets a big smile on his face. "Then comes football. Football is great because it's a team sport. When you play football, you're on the field with ten other guys, working together. Running onto the field with your team, playing together with those other guys on the field, and winning… it's the most powerful feeling in the world. When we won that state championship our sophomore year, it was unbelievable."

I scratch my head, trying to make sense of his answers. I would have bet my life savings, which isn't much, that wrestling was his favorite sport. I would do anything to be so good at any sport. "So, football is your favorite?"

Woody asks, "Honestly?"

"Well yeah, honestly."

"Honestly, my favorite sport is basketball." Now Woody is beaming. "I'm only five-six and one hundred and forty-five pounds, but I love basketball. I love filling the lane on a fast break. I love playing defense and shutting down my opponent. I'm tenacious on defense." He smiles. "Plus, there's the team aspect. You have closer friendships than what you would have on the football team, less guys."

As Woody digs into another wing, I copy down another surprising response into my notebook.

I write <u>BASKETBALL?</u>, put a question mark next to it, and then underline it.

Woody puts his fist to his chest and tries to catch his breath.

"You all right?" I ask.

"Must be a little heart burn," he says. "Maybe I should ease up on the wings."

"If you love basketball so much, why didn't you play?"

"It goes back to middle school. Our 7th grade team went undefeated, but I didn't see eye to eye with my 8th grade coach. So, I wrestled." Woody shrugs his shoulders. "I found out that I was good at it. Freshman year, my season was cut short because of an ankle injury. Sophomore year, I only wrestled fifteen matches, until I broke my thumb, but I won all fifteen at the varsity level. I knew I was good, and that I just needed to stay healthy and put an entire season together. My junior year, I went 31-2 and won the state championship."

"So you had reached your goal."

Woody points at me and says, "Exactly, I won a Division I State Championship. I had won at the highest level. I didn't have anything to prove to anybody. So this year, I tried out for the basketball team."

This news nearly knocks me out of my seat. "You did what?"

"Yeah," Woody chuckles to himself, "the varsity basketball coach told me he couldn't keep me, that the town would have his head on a platter. Everyone knew we had a shot at winning a team state championship in wrestling, the first one in the history of the school."

"Do you think you had a legitimate shot to make the basketball team? Would you have deserved a spot on the team?"

Woody nods his head. "I think I could have helped the team win."

"Wow, but you wrestled instead?" I ask, shaking my head in disbelief.

"Coach D pulled me into his office, explained that this team had a chance to make history, to make our school the best in the state. We could have a team state championship."

"And get a sign on all four corners of the city."

Woody says, "Yeah, something like that."

"What was your record this year?"

"Funny enough, same record as last year, 31-2 in the regular season."

I copy down the record on my notepad. "What about the state tournament? How did you win a team title this year?"

Woody wipes his hands on a napkin. "We had enough guys qualify for the tournament, and we just needed them to place high enough to get points."

"And you needed to win another title."

"Coach D told me I needed to pin all the way through to get enough points."

"You get more points if you win by a pin?"

Nodding his head, Woody says, "Yeah, I had a sixteen man draw. Four total matches. In order to get enough points, I had to pin all the way to the finals."

"But you didn't pin your opponent in the finals."

"Major decision. And a state championship for the city."

"Did you know you could win the last match?"

Woody grits his teeth together, like he's reliving the moment. "I saw the kid after he won his semifinal match. I stared him down. I could see in his eyes that he wanted nothing to do with me. He was just happy to be in the finals. I won the match before we even got on the mat. Maybe it was the Mohawk." Woody rubs his head and smiles.

"What was the best part about winning?"

"Thinking back to the day my brother won. How I told myself that one day I would be a state champion, and I did it." Looking up toward the ceiling, Woody says, "You know what, the best part was the day after. I took my German Shepard to the Metro Parks. I drove him up in my car, and we ran in this big open field. He played fetch. I sat down in the grass, and he licked my face. We spent the entire day together. I could finally breathe a sigh of relief. All the pressure was off. The city had a state championship, and I was done with wrestling."

"What are you most proud of?"

"People don't know what it takes to be a state champion or win a state championship. Most guys just go to practice, and do what the coaches tell them, but that's not enough. You have to be willing to make the ultimate sacrifices. Running extra, more time in the weight room, and the courage to face any kind of opponent. It's just you and your opponent on the mat. It's all about who is going to back down first. Sometimes, it's not even about how good of a wrestler you are. It's about heart. It's about who wants it more. I wanted that first state championship more than anything because no one thought I could do it. I was the under-dog, and I proved everyone wrong. And the second one was awesome, and not just for myself, but for the city, and Coach D." Woody grabs his chest again.

"You all right?" I ask.

"Yeah, yeah, I'm fine. Must be the wings," he says again.

"You mentioned earlier that sometimes you feel like a racehorse. Do you feel that it's really like that?"

"Sometimes, I feel like that, but I wouldn't trade anything in the world for the feeling of winning a state championship. When you're exhausted, and it's the third period, and you feel like a heavy-weight-boxing-champion, wondering what you're made of, hoping you won't slip. But there's nothing like find-ing something deep inside yourself that says I am stronger than my opponent. I've worked harder. I de-serve this more. So you find this part of yourself that is completely fearless and willing to take on anyone at any time. It's then that the sport takes on a dif-ferent meaning. In fact, it doesn't matter what the sport is; it's the competition. It's you against another human being. It's all about finding out what you're made of. And then, standing on that center mat in front of your friends and family and your town as the best wrestler in the state, there's nothing like it. I can't imagine anything better than that. Even though I wear our school's name on the front of my uniform, I wrestled for me."

Wow. Woody's speech has my blood pumping. I feel like I can take on the world. In more ways than one, I am inspired. Looking down my list of questions, I ask, "Are you going to wrestle in college?"

Woody shakes his head and says, "Notre Dame, Penn State, and Iowa have all offered me scholarships, but my wrestling days are over."

I am taken aback by this unexpected answer. I figured he would have used wrestling if for nothing else a free education. "Over?" I ask. "How can someone so good at something just walk away from it?"

"I think because it's so individual. You can't share a wrestling championship the same way you can share a victory with your friends on the football field or the basketball court. When you win with your friends, there's a connection that you have with those guys, a brotherhood."

Busily, I copy down Woody's answer. I am both amazed and confused by Woody not pursuing a Division I scholarship. So I ask, "Where are you thinking about going to school?"

"Mount Union. It's close to home. Division III football. The coaches think I can play there."

"No hoops?"

"Not many colleges looking for a five foot six point guard." Woody laughs to himself and wipes his hands with a napkin.

I write down Basketball :) again and put a smiley face next to it. Continuing with the interview, I ask, "So now that graduation is right around the corner, what are you going to do this summer?"

"Put on some weight for football season. Football season starts in a few months, and I want to be in the best shape of my life. The coach told me I needed to put on some weight to play football. It will be interesting to put on weight and get in shape at the same time."

"What position are you going to try out for?"

"Probably running back or wing back. I have good speed, so it will make up for my lack of size."

"I wish you all the luck in the world at Mount Union. I'm sure you'll do great there."

"Thanks, George. I appreciate it."

As I sit across the table from Woody Fletcher, I think about the interview. I think about what it's like to be in the presence of true greatness. Woody has a depth to him that I never would have anticipated or expected. I can honestly say that I feel that I am better for having had the experience of sitting down and talking to Woody Fletcher. Extending my hand across the table, I say, "Thanks for taking the time to come and talk to me about your season, and sharing a little bit about your life."

Woody shakes my hand and says, "It was my pleasure. It was fun, a little trip down memory lane. When are you going to run the story?"

"It will be in the last issue of the school newspaper before we graduate. I'll send you a rough draft to make sure you're good with everything."

"Sounds good, George."

After paying the bill, we walk out into the parking lot. Woody stops me and says, "Something's been bothering me about my answer to one of your questions. When you asked me who influenced me the most, I said my dad. Can I change that answer?"

I stop and look at Woody. "Of course you can. I haven't written anything yet," I say.

Woody gets this look of satisfaction and peace. He says, "Without a doubt, it was my mom. She taught me how powerful love can be. I love Coach D. I love my buddies on the wrestling team. When I said I wrestled for me, that was true, but no doubt I wrestled for them as well. I love my brothers. But my mom, she's just about the most amazing woman I know." Woody pauses and then says, "My mom never missed a match. She has been the one constant in my life, through the good and the bad. She's the one that has made the biggest difference."

This part of the interview I don't need to write down. In fact, Woody's sincerity has created a moment that I will never forget. Looking at Woody I say, "I will be sure to make the change in my notes."

With a look of relief, Woody says, "Thanks, George. I appreciate it."

Woody jumps in his rusted out SUV, and I get into my beat up Toyota and drive home to type the story.

That night I start working on the interview with Woody. I try to think about what parts of the story would be the most interesting to my classmates. His motivation? His will to win? His fear of failure? The fact that he wanted to play basketball?! I'm not sure where to start, so my computer screen remains blank. Despite my best intentions, I don't get anything down.

Over the next couple days, I am not able to get anything done on my story. Plus, I don't see Woody in school, so I decide to call over to his house.

His mom answers the phone. "Hello?"

"Hi, Mrs. Fletcher. This is George Miller. I noticed that Woody hasn't been in school the last couple of days. Is he okay?"

"He's okay, George. He's sleeping right now. He went into the hospital for chest pain a couple days ago. The x-rays showed that he has an enlarged heart. We thought it would be best to keep him out of school for a couple days."

"An enlarged heart?" I repeat.

"The doctors say he has an arrhythmia because of the size of his heart. They say he will be fine. He might have to take some medication."

For a moment, I am speechless on the other end of the line. "I'm glad he's okay, Mrs. Fletcher. I'll try calling back later. Would you let him know that I called?"

"It was nice of you to call," she says. "I'll let him know."

I hang up the phone and look at the wall and think about my conversation with Woody. I think about Secretariat, and I think about what it takes to be a champion.

An enlarged heart... I'm not surprised.

When I sit down to write the story about Woody, I Google: Quotes from famous wrestlers.

A quote from the Olympic Champion Dan Gable pops up on the screen: "The 1st period is won by the best technician. The 2nd period is won by the kid in the best shape. The 3rd period is won by the kid with the biggest heart."

Thinking about the quote, I realize that Woody Fletcher had it all. He was a technician. Coach D had taught him the technical side of the sport. He was better conditioned. He was in better shape than anyone he faced because he outworked his opponent. But most importantly, he had more heart than anybody on the mat. I try to think about how in the short time I spent with Woody Fletcher I was inspired.

Woody taught me about getting a goal in your sights and pursuing that goal relentlessly, and with passion, and most importantly, without fear. I've always wanted to be a journalist, and my conversation with Woody has inspired me to pursue my own dream of becoming a journalist. He showed me that if I wanted something bad enough, I had to go out and get it, work hard to get it, despite the fear of failure.

Right then, I know what my story is going to be about. I type the title of my story:

Heart of a Champion

I continue to type the body of the story:

> Ohio has some of the best high school wrestling in the country, and today, I have the opportunity to interview one of the toughest, most feared, two-time state champions, Woody Fletcher.

Questions on *Heart of a Champion*:

A flat character is one dimensional and not well developed. A round character is a well-developed character that is multi-dimensional. A static character remains essentially the same over the course of the story, and a dynamic character changes from the beginning to the end of the story.

1. Some stories are driven by a strong plot. Others are driven by characters. This is clearly a story driven by characters. A round character is well developed and someone the reader knows a lot about. What parts of the story demonstrate the depth of the character of Woody Fletcher? What makes Woody a character that is round in this story?

    Give textual evidence that supports Woody being a round/ multidimensional character:

    _____

    _____

    _____

    _____

    _____

    _____

    _____

    _____

    _____

2. A dynamic character changes over the course of the story. Would you consider George Miller a dynamic character? Explain why or why not.

_____

_____

_____

_____

_____

_____

_____

_____

_____

_____

_____

_____

_____

_____

_____

_____

_____

_____

SPRING

BASEBALL: THE FINAL INNING

"Every day is a new opportunity. You can build on yesterday's success or put its failures behind and start over again. That's the way life is, with a new game every day, and that's the way baseball is."
—Bob Feller
(Major League Pitcher)

It's June 2nd, the day of the Ohio High School State Championship baseball game. Sweat pours from the head of our starting pitcher, Ryan Jackson. He takes off his hunter-green hat and wipes the sweat from his forehead. The sun sits high in the afternoon sky. There is not a cloud to shield our pitcher from the heat. The stands are packed with fans wearing the blue and gold from Cincinnati Moeller, and the fans from our school are wearing the green and white of the Mayfield Wildcats. The player from Moeller steps out of the batter's box and adjusts his batting gloves. He looks down the line at his third base coach and tugs on the front of his helmet to indicate that he has received the sign. Then he steps back into the batter's box.

We are up 1-0 at the start of the bottom of the last inning. Ryan has pitched a gem. He's had the hitters on Moeller's baseball team guessing all day. He's had every pitch working, from the placement of his fast-ball to his curveball to his ridiculous slider. But after throwing over 100 pitches in the humidity, his fatigue is starting to show.

Ryan rears back and fires a slider that misses the strike zone. "Ball four," grunts the stout umpire from behind home plate. "Take your base."

When they get their first base runner of the inning, Coach Hayes strokes his gray beard, spits out a few sunflower seeds, looks over at me and in a hoarse voice says, "Frankie, go get warmed up. We might need you to close this thing."

Nodding my head, I grab my buddy, Pete. We walk behind the fence next to the dugout and start warming up. My arm feels great, and from my position behind the fence, I can see that Ryan's arm is starting to fail him. He's lost the velocity on his pitches, and his curveball isn't breaking like it should.

Quickly, Ryan is struggling. He's down 2-0 in the count to the next batter. The players from Cincinnati Moeller have stopped helping Ryan out by swinging at pitches outside the strike zone. They have started to make Ryan throw strikes, and in the last inning of the game, he's having a difficult time finding the zone.

After I've warmed my arm up, Pete crouches down in the catcher's position. I begin to throw a little bit harder. The ball releases from my hand and smacks into Pete's catcher's mitt. I love that sound. Even though I'm not pitching right now in the game, my heart starts to pound, and the adrenaline begins to race through my body.

"Ball three!" shouts the umpire from the other side of the fence.

My nervousness begins to set in. Everybody thinks that being a closer is the easiest job in the world. One inning. That's it. That's all you have to pitch. Three outs. Game over. The problem is it's usually in the closest of games, two runs or less. When you're a closer, there is no room for error.

"Ball four! Take your base!" shouts the umpire.

Moeller has a man on first and second with no outs. I'm hoping that Coach Hayes will put me in now. That will give me at least one base to play with. Coach calls to me from the corner of the dugout. "Frankie, I'm going to give Ryan one more batter. He's earned that with the game he's pitched. If he walks the next batter, you're up."

"Yes, sir," I say. And he's right. Ryan has earned the right to pitch to the next batter. He's pitched a hell of game. But coming into a game with bases loaded and no outs is a nightmare. There is no safety net.

Smack. I fire another fastball into Pete's glove, and he shakes his hand, indicating that one stung. "You've got your stuff today. No doubt about it," says Pete.

"Ball one," calls the ump.

The crowd from Mayfield groans. They understand that Ryan has pitched an unbelievable game. Six scoreless innings. They want to give Ryan a chance to pitch the shutout, but they also want to win a state championship.

On the very next pitch, the batter steps into one of Ryan's fastballs and crushes the ball down the left field line. The ball soars high into the air. All eyes are focused on the ball as it takes flight toward the home run fence. This can be the game. I hold my breath. The ball climbs higher and higher, but at the last second, it drifts left of the foul pole.

"Foul ball! Strike one. One and one," says the ump, as he tosses another ball to Ryan on the pitcher's mound. Everyone on our side of the bleachers and in our dugout lets out a collective sigh of relief. We are one pitch away from losing the game.

"Just a long strike," says a relieved Coach Hayes from the dugout, clapping his hands.

Ryan shakes his head and shoots me a look that says—get me out of here. The last swing of the bat almost cost us a state championship, our last chance as seniors.

Ryan's next two pitches aren't even close. He walks the bases loaded. He doesn't want to come out of the game. That's not how competitors are built, but he knows he doesn't have anything left in the tank. So here we are, bottom of the seventh, bases loaded, no outs.

Coach Hayes jogs out to the mound. He puts his arm around Ryan. Whispers something to him. Then he motions for me to come into the game to close it out.

Pete says, "Gun 'em down, Frankie." He gives me a high five as I jog around the fence and onto the field.

On the pitcher's mound are Coach Hayes, Ryan, and our catcher, Will Webber. Ryan lets out a deep breath and smiles, knowing he's off the hook.

"Sorry about the bases loaded deal. I guess it's better than the ball sitting on the other side of the home-run fence," says Ryan, shrugging his shoulders.

Will smiles and sarcastically says, "Yeah, it's not like he's leaving you with the meat of the order: 3, 4, and 5."

Coach Hayes says, "Ryan, you pitched a heck of a game, son." Then he looks at me. "But that's what you've got kid. You've got their best hitters. But they don't know how good you can be. They don't know what you're made of. How you can rise to the challenge." The intensity in his voice has my adrenaline flowing like a steady stream.

"Yes, sir," I say, thinking back to our travel team. Will, Ryan and I have played together since we were eight years old, almost ten years. We've had similar discussions before. We've always had each other's backs, and now it's my turn to have Ryan's. The role of helping my friend gives me unprecedented strength.

Coach Hayes takes the ball from Ryan's mitt and plunks it into the web of my glove. "Listen, it's just you and Will now, just you and the catcher's mitt. That's all you need to think about. Find the zone and stay there. Can you do that?"

"Yes, sir," I say.

A look of pure determination stretches across Coach's face. "Listen kid, this is the opportunity of a lifetime. It's an opportunity to show how much character you've got. How fearless you are. Do your best.

And no matter what, remember… have fun. When it's all said and done, it's just a game." He looks at me and smiles.

"Let's go, Coach," says the umpire. "Time's up. Your pitcher has eight pitches to warm up, and then we gotta go."

Coach Hayes pats me on the back. "Let's go, kid. Show 'em what you've got."

Ryan raises his hand for fist bump. "Bail me out," he says. "Three outs from a state championship. Don't even think about the base runners. They aren't going anywhere."

Ryan and Coach Hayes jog off the field, leaving Will and me on the pitcher's mound.

Will smiles, pats me on the back and says, "This is your chance to be the hero."

"Yeah, or the goat," I say.

"Listen man, I've been catching you for ten years. Bring the heat, bring the breaking ball, and throw that cutter when you need to. It's your best pitch." Will slides his catcher's mask over his face and jogs back to home plate.

I fire my eight warm-up pitches, and my arm feels great. The ball feels good coming out of my hand, and my legs feel strong. The ball pops in Will's mitt. When I catch the ball, I look into the stands. They are filled with our entire town, except for one person that is missing, my dad. I resent my dad for not being at the most important game of my life. He said he need-ed to get sober, and that was the most important thing. That he had to put himself first. That's what he's been doing this past couple weeks. He tried to explain that if he wasn't sober, he wasn't good to anybody. I didn't understand that at the time. It was my own selfishness. In many ways, I am just like my dad.

"Batter up," calls the umpire.

When I catch the ball from Will, I walk to the other side of the pitcher's mound. Rubbing the ball with my hands, I start to think. I always wondered what pitchers thought about while they were on the pitcher's mound in the middle of a World Series. Or what a quarterback thought about on the final drive in the fourth quarter of a Super Bowl. I always thought it would be just the moment itself. But for me, in the biggest moment of my life, I'm not even thinking about the moment. I'm thinking about something that is much more important to me. I'm thinking about my dad, two hours away, at University Hospital. He checked himself in two weeks ago, just when our run to the state championship started. He was all the way in the bag when he called his brother to pick him up and take him to treatment.

It's then that the strangest thing happens. When I step onto the pitcher's mound, I don't see Will crouched behind home plate. Instead, in my mind, I see my dad when I was ten years old. He's crouched behind the plate, playing catcher, helping to get me to throw strikes. Physically, I am on the pitcher's mound in the state championship baseball game facing a bases loaded bottom of the seventh with no outs, but in my mind, I'm in a completely different place.

Peering over the web of my glove, I pretend I'm the three-time Cy Young award winner, Pedro Martinez.

He has by far the most intimidating look. He has the eyes that barely look over his glove, staring down his opponent. My eyes narrow and look in to see Will's signal. I smell the leather of the glove, and think about the time my dad took me to watch the Cleveland Indians play at Progressive Field. I remember my dad telling me to watch the pitcher's mechanics. More importantly, he told me to watch how the pitcher's emotions never changed. He explained that you can have all kinds of emotions going on inside, but on the outside, you have to keep it together. Don't show any chinks in the armor.

Will wants the fastball. I rear back and fire a fastball right down the pipe. The ball explodes in Will's mitt for a strike, and the dust from his mitt shoots into the air. Even I am surprised by the velocity of my fastball. Looking into the batter's eyes, I know that I have him. His wide eyes show that he knows he's in serious trouble. He's probably wondering how he's going to catch up with that pitch.

Again my mind drifts to all of my little league games and travel teams that my dad coached. My favorite parts of those games were never the games themselves. What I remember most was that my dad and I would always arrive an hour before the game started. And we would play catch. It was always just me and my dad, like two best friends. My mom and sister would show up when the game started, but that hour was what I treasured. We would talk about everything under the sun: baseball, school, and girls… and anything else that was on my mind.

Will flashes two fingers from between his legs, the sign for the curveball.

After nodding my head to okay the sign, I go into my pitching motion. Snapping my wrist, the ball takes flight directly toward the batter. He leans out of the way, just as my curve breaks across and out of the strike zone.

"Ball one," calls the umpire. "One and one is the count."

Will zips the ball back to me. When I catch the ball, I tuck my mitt under my arm and rub the sweat from my hands into the ball, softening it up.

Our shortstop, Jimmy Court says, "Let's go, Frankie. Finish 'em off."

I give Jimmy the thumbs up and then slip my glove back on and face the batter. The other runners are taking their leads, dancing around, trying to distract me. I think back to playing catch with my dad. He would create a scenario like this: no outs, bottom of the seventh. He would get in the catcher's position, and he would make me pretend it was the real thing. I had to make the perfect pitch when I needed to. "Remember," he used to say, "don't worry about the base runners. It's just you and the catcher's mitt. Just you and the mitt."

Will positions himself behind home plate and then lowers a single finger, indicating fastball.

I shake my head, waving him off.

In the middle of my trying to get the sign, the third base coach calls to the their batter, and the batter steps out of the box to look down at his coach. He nods to his coach, and I motion to Will. We know they have a play on, but we don't know what it is. We know the runner at third base has great speed, but because

Moeller has not been able to manufacture any runs, a suicide squeeze is not out of the question.

Will drops three fingers for the cutter, my best pitch. I go into my pitching motion. Just as I release the ball, the runner from third base starts sprinting down the line. My pitch, which is supposed to be low and away, instead, goes inside.

The batter puts his bat out for a bunt, and the suicide squeeze is on. The ball is deadened off the bat and rolls down the third base line. If the ball gets past me, the run will score for sure, and the game will be tied.

I dive to my right and stop the ball with my bare hand, and getting to my knees, I fire the ball to Will, who has home plate blocked. The runner from third lowers his shoulder right into Will, just like Pete Rose's famous play at the plate in the All-Star game with Ray Fosse. The runner bowls Will over, and a giant cloud of dust swirls around home plate for what seems like an eternity. When the dust finally clears, Will holds the ball up in his mitt, showing that he has held on to the ball for the out.

The umpire pumps his fist. "Out at home!" shouts the umpire.

Will tosses the ball to me and says, "Nice play, Frankie!"

"Way to go!" I say, patting him on the shoulder and heading back to the mound. We still need two more outs.

Cincinnati Moeller's cleanup hitter slides the weight off his bat and heads to the batter's box. Knocking the dirt from his cleats, he takes a couple practice cuts. This six foot four inch monster has gone three for three on the day. He's easily their toughest out. I know my pitches have to be perfect. Each pitch will have to paint the corner. My approach to this hitter will be different than the first. I might throw a couple out of the zone, just to keep him honest. But I don't have much room to play around. A walk ties the game.

Checking the signals from Will, I think about how my dad injured his shoulder. We came from the Dominican Republic. He came here to pitch for the Lake County Captains, a minor league team for Cleveland. He was having an amazing season, leading the team in innings pitched and an ERA of 1.23. The Indians were thinking about bringing him up to The Show. But half way through the season, he tore his rotator cuff. Because his shoulder never healed right, he never pitched again. He was forced to find work at a factory in downtown Cleveland. My dad has never been the same.

I start off with a curveball that dives low into the dirt. "Ball one," says the umpire.

When I get the ball back from Will, I think about the day my dad came home after he had been laid off from the factory. I've never seen him more disappointed. Fifteen years on the line at the factory, and they let him go. Said the economy was crumbling. He tried to explain to me all about supply and demand. I didn't understand. Fifteen years of loyalty, never missing a day. Doesn't that trump supply and demand?

Will lowers both hands slowly, indicating that I need to slow down, compose myself. He flashes one finger for the fastball.

Instead of calming down, I work quickly, winding up and firing another fastball that almost flies over Will's head. He has to stand up to catch the ball, saving me from a wild pitch and a run scored.

"Ball two. 2-0 is the count," says the umpire.

Will says something to the umpire and then jogs out to the mound. Covering his mouth with his catcher's mitt, he says, "C'mon, man. That ball almost got by me. Let's go, Frankie. You're already behind on this kid, and you definitely don't want to go 3-0. He knows you have to come to him. Throw the cutter, low and on the outside part of the plate. You know you can put it right where you want it. You've done it a million times."

"I know. I know," I say.

Looking at me, Will says, "You all right, man. Looks like you're someplace else."

Shaking my head, I say, "No, no, I'm good."

"Let's go, man. *Weather the storm*," says Will, as he pats me on the back and heads back to home plate.

Weather the storm. That's what my dad kept saying. For six months, we weathered the storm, while my dad looked for another job, and my mom did some part-time work. My dad is the proudest man I know, and not being able to support his family was literally killing him. I think he began drinking to ease the pain. Once the drinking began, soon after, came the deepest depression.

My next pitch is the cutter. The ball heads right toward Will's glove, right where he wants it. Their number four hitter takes a healthy cut at the pitch, and he fouls it straight back. The ball rattles against the backstop. He's right on my best pitch.

"Foul ball. Strike one," calls the umpire. "Two and one."

Will jogs back to get the foul ball and throws it back to me and says, "That a boy, Frankie. Good pitch."

Their cleanup hitter is going to be hard to strike out. I think about the advice my dad gave me. Rely on your teammates. You can't do everything yourself. Of course, my dad never took his own advice. Our family was our team, and he wouldn't let anyone help him. He was too proud.

Will calls for the cutter again.

I shake my head.

He calls for the curve.

I shake my head.

Finally, he calls for the heater.

A fastball low in the zone creates grounders. The fewer pitches I throw to their best hitter, the better. Rearing back, I fire a fastball low and inside. Their cleanup batter steps into the pitch and smacks a blue dart between shortstop and third base. The crowd goes silent as all the base runners are in motion. Jimmy Court sprints to his left and makes a diving stop, just like the great Omar Vizquel. Because of the velocity of the hit, Jimmy still has a play at home. He fires a laser to Will at home plate. The ball smacks into Will's mitt just before the runner from third base crosses home.

The umpire raises his fist into the air. "Out!" he thunders.

Our fans jump to their feet and cheer, and the Moeller fans let out noises like they've been shot. But no one disagrees with the call. It was a bang-bang play, but it was clear that the ball had reached Will's mitt before the runner had touched home.

"Two outs," says the umpire.

Will jogs out to the mound and places the ball inside my mitt. He lets out a deep breath and says, "Wow, that was close. I told you to go with cutter."

"How many outs are there?" I say.

Will smiles, lets out a deep breath, and says, "Two."

I smile real big at Will and say, "What are you worried about?" Taking my hat off, I wipe the sweat from my forehead and let out a deep breath of my own.

Will looks at me and says, "Let's go fastball. This batter had trouble catching up with Ryan's fastball, and yours has more pop than his today." Before Will heads back to home plate he says, "Listen, one out and we're done. State champs. What we've always dreamed about."

Funny how your dreams change when your dad loses his job and checks himself into rehab. How your priorities change. Strange how what used to be really important, takes a backseat. But I know how much this means to my friends, and I would never let them down. And based on Jimmy's effort on that last play, I know they would never let me down.

Settling in on the pitcher's mound, I check the runners on the bases. I reach back with everything I have, and I fire a fastball right down the pipe.

Their batter takes a cut, but almost a second too late as the ball sits in Will's mitt. When Will tosses the ball back to the pitcher's mound, I think again about my dad, sitting in a hospital room, going to therapy sessions, making collages about how he feels and the regret he has. Visiting him yesterday, I think back to the collage that he made that sat next to his bed. It was loaded with words he cut out from a magazine that somehow illustrated his feelings: FEAR, SHAME, GUILT, and REGRET. The list of words went on and on, in different directions across the giant piece of paper. Like he needed a huge piece of paper to remind him of all the things he's done wrong.

Leaning in for the sign, Will calls for another fastball. I stand up tall and go into my set position. I throw a fastball low and away, that catches the bottom of the strike zone.

"Strike two," says the umpire.

Our crowd shouts and cheers. They can taste the victory.

The Cincinnati Moeller crowd moans. They are down to their last strike.

Up 0-2 in the count, I know I have the batter right where I want him. I can waste two pitches if I want. Make him chase, without any risk of having him get anything on the ball.

Will calls for the cutter.

The next pitch looks like it's exactly where I want it. The ball seems to fly in slow motion. It's almost as if I can see the laces on the ball catch the wind and break toward Will's mitt. The batter never takes his bat off his shoulder. The ball is low on the outside corner of the plate. The perfect pitch smacks into Will's mitt.

"Ball one!" calls the umpire.

Standing frozen on the mound, I look at Will's mitt as he frames the pitch, just inside the strike zone. *That was strike three*, I say to myself. That was the pitch that should have won us a state championship.

Is that the luck in my family? No breaks for Frankie or his father?

Our fans shout in disbelief, and the Moeller fans cheer, knowing they're still alive.

When I get the ball from Will, I am shaken.

The game should be over.

We should be state champs.

Instead of stepping off the mound and composing myself, I peer in for the signal from Will.

He calls for a curveball.

My rage is as much for the bad call as it is for my dad losing his job. Much of the anger comes from seeing my dad lose his identity.

I throw the curve. The ball breaks too early. It skips in the dirt and takes off toward the backstop. While I sprint forward to cover home plate, Will slides to his right almost three feet to stop the ball, saving the run from coming home from third base.

Will barely manages to get in front of the wild pitch. The runner from third is almost halfway down the line. Will holds the ball up and chases the runner down the line, and the runner retreats safely back to third.

Will shakes his head and tosses the ball back to me. "C'mon, Frankie. Let's go." The frustration rumbles in his voice.

Stepping off the pitcher's mound, I look around at the stands, and look at the families that have come out to support us. Then I look at our dugout and all the players on our team. This is what we've always dreamed about, the opportunity of a lifetime. Jimmy's voice cuts into my thoughts. "One pitch, Frankie. One time. Let's go."

Nodding to Jimmy, I step onto the mound and look in for the sign from Will.

He signals fastball, and I know it's the right pitch to throw. Rearing back, I make sure this pitch is not outside for Will. The pitch is straight, but it rises, like it's climbing stairs. The batter holds off of the pitch and checks his swing.

"Ball three!" calls the umpire. "Full count."

Will calls time and jogs out to the mound.

Before Will even gets to the mound, I say, "That pitch at 0-2 was a strike," I say. "The game should be over. I can't believe he called that a ball." Staring at Will, I say, "Now I've got bases loaded… It's the last inning, and I've got a full count. I've got no choice but to bring it to him."

"Not completely," says Will, "let's go with the fastball. You can make the pitch, and he's got to swing at anything close. He's not going home with a backwards K on his final bat of the state championship. If he hits it, you've a got a great team behind you. They can make plays."

"Yeah, yeah, you're right," I say, glancing at my teammates behind me.

"Let's go, Frankie. You can do this," says Will, as he slides his mask over his face and turns to head back to home plate.

So this is it. One pitch for an entire season, and a lifetime, I think to myself. I think cutter, but I know that pitch has to be perfect. My curveball has been less than accurate. I know the right pitch to throw is the fastball. It has the best chance of finding the strike zone, and Will is right, he's going to swing at anything close. And if he does hit it, we've got a great defense.

Will gets set behind home plate. The batter digs his cleats into the dirt, and takes a few practice swings. I let out a couple deep breaths to compose myself. I look in for the sign.

Fastball.

I nod my head.

All I can think is that I need to throw a pitch that will make the batter have to win the game. I can't throw a ball out of the strike zone to walk in the tying run. The ball sails from my hand, but instead of throwing one of my good fastballs, I push a pitch that hangs up in the middle of the zone. A big old watermelon.

The batter's eyes light up. He steps into the pitch and crushes the ball. I turn to follow its flight. It soars toward right center field. Our center fielder, Anthony Miller, turns and opens up toward the ball, jumping on his horse. The ball is heading toward the fence, but Anthony doesn't give up on it. He takes the perfect angle, and I know that Anthony, the ball, and the fence will all meet at the same moment.

Just as the ball is about to clear the fence, Anthony jumps onto the fence, and climbs up it with one push from his left foot. He slides his mitt over the top of the fence and catches the ball, robbing the batter of a home-run and Cincinnati Moeller of a state championship.

I drop my head in relief, and then turn to see Will sprinting toward me with arms wide open. We hug, and the dugout clears. The infielders run toward us, and when Anthony sprints in from center field with the ball safely in his mitt, the celebration begins. Ryan jumps on me. Jimmy and the rest of the infield jump on Will, causing a large pile of players right in front of the pitcher's mound. The shouting and cheering pervade the stadium. We are on top of the world. Mayfield has won the Ohio High School State Championship.

After our ten-minute celebration, we shake hands with the players from a disappointed Moeller team, and then we get hugs and high fives from friends and family.

There is a big trophy celebration. Moeller is presented their second place trophy, and then we get to hold up our state championship trophy. I can only imagine that every player on our team feels like they are on top of the world.

Except for me. I can't stop thinking about my dad.

Coach Hayes brings the team together and gives an emotional speech about what an unbelievable journey our team has been on. How we battled back all season. How we never gave up. How it has been a privilege to coach one of the most "hard-working" and "cohesive" groups he has ever been a part of. He tells us to keep this moment in our hearts. He gives away two game balls. One goes to Ryan for his six innings of unbelievable pitching, and he gives the other one to me. He tells our team that we will remember this moment for the rest of our lives.

Once we board the bus, we settle in for a three-hour drive back to school. The other players on the team laugh and joke the entire way home, celebrating our victory. For the first five minutes, I join in, but then I grab my phone, select a playlist, and put my earbuds in and think about my dad. I consider all the things I want to say to him, how I know that he's doing what he needs to do to get better. I know that my dad has the same spirit as our team. He has the will to battle back and the desire to never give up.

After the bus pulls into the parking lot at school, Coach Hayes says, "Pizza party paid for by the coaches. The whole team should meet at Carlo's Pizza in about an hour."

I have other plans. With my cleats still on, I climb in my car with one destination in mind: University Hospital.

The hospital is in downtown Cleveland. Driving through the city, I hit some traffic, but I eventually arrive at the parking garage of the hospital. I grab my baseball bag and make my way to the front desk and then up the elevator.

When I get to my dad's room, he looks up from his chair. He is watching, what else, an Indian's game. He has lost a lot of weight, and he looks much smaller. He has drifted down to his rock bottom. But putting on your best face is something my dad has taught me. Don't show any chinks in the armor.

A wide smile stretches across his unshaven face. "So, how'd it go?" he asks.

With a dust covered uniform, I say, "We won."

"Ah, that's my boy." He gets up from his chair and gives me a big hug.

"How are you?" I ask.

My dad waves me off. Always pretending things are better than they really are. "Oh, you know, I'm gettin' better. One day at a time," he says this with an embarrassed smile.

I nod my head.

Looking down at my bag, my dad asks, "What did you bring?"

He knows too well what the bag holds—my mitt and a catcher's mitt.

I just smile.

"Let me get my shoes on," he says.

We take the elevator downstairs and walk outside to an open patch of grass. After handing him the catcher's mitt, we stand about twenty feet apart. And slowly, we begin to toss the ball, the game ball, back and forth.

"Well," my dad says taking the ball out of his glove and throwing it back to me, "I want to hear all about it." The tears are welling up in his eyes.

Catching his throw, I say, "Bases loaded. The final inning. No outs. Coach Hayes sends me in." I toss the ball back to my dad.

My dad catches the ball and smiles. "Ha, how 'bout that. Just like we practiced."

"Yeah, just like we practiced," I say. Looking at my dad, I say, "Coach gave one game ball to Ryan, and I got the other one."

"That must have been something." My dad examines the ball and tosses it back to me. "I want you to know I was with you. I was with you the whole time."

Funny thing is, he was with me the entire time. During that last inning, all I could think about was my dad and what he means to me. I know that no matter what happens to my dad, he will always be with me. I will always have his unconditional love, and he will always have mine.

Catching the ball in my glove, I have this thought: The best part about this day, the thing I will remember more than anything, will not be the state championship baseball game, or even getting the game ball for that matter, but rather, I will remember playing catch with my dad. When I think about what my dad said about being with me the whole time, I look up and say, "I know you were, dad. I know you were."

Questions on *The Final Inning*:

1. Point of view is extremely important in a story.
   This story is told in first person from the point of
   view of Frankie. Explain how this story would
   be different if it was told from the third person
   limited or third person omniscient point of view.
   Would the emotion be different? Would the story
   be as effective? What if the story was told from
   the father's point of view as he listened to the
   game on the radio?

_____

_____

_____

_____

_____

_____

_____

_____

_____

_____

_____

_____

_____

_____

TRACK: MOVING FORWARD

"We just have one basic focus. We're focused on going one direction, and that's forward."

—Michael Johnson
(Olympic Gold Medalist)

The crowd is silent in the Jesse Owens Memorial Stadium in downtown Columbus. The sun is blocked by black and gray storm clouds. I look up into the heavens and think about my best friend, Terry Witherspoon. There is no doubt he is up there and looking down on us today, expecting greatness from each and every one of us. This was his dream, our dream. Today, it is our job to make this dream come true. The spectators look on with quiet anticipation for the beginning of the Division I, 4 X 400 meter championship, the final race in this year's Ohio High

School State Track meet. They always save the best for last. The 4 X 400 brings out the best in everyone. The race requires it all: strategy, strength, endurance, speed, teamwork, and fearlessness.

My blood pumps hard, and my anxiety makes my knees feel rubbery, wobbly.

The deep voice of the starter thunders and pierces the silence. "Runners to your mark!" He raises one hand.

Seven other runners from the other Division I schools prepare for the biggest race of their lives. The runners in the other lanes kick their legs out and stretch quads and hamstrings. They tilt their heads from side to side in anticipation. Each runner, like the scene itself, is electric.

Treyvon Johnson, the first leg of our relay, slides his right foot up against the starting block in lane #4. He kicks out his left foot, getting loose. He lines his fingers up, flat against the starting line. I position my foot on the back of his starting block to steady it, so it doesn't slip. In this race, a fraction of a second can be the difference between winning and losing. In fact, I've learned over the last couple of months that just about everything in life comes down to hours, minutes, and seconds.

"Get set!" The starter raises his starting gun.

The first runner from each team elevates to their starting position.

Treyvon lifts up in his starting blocks.

"BANG!" The gun fires.

Treyvon explodes out of his starting block, pushing hard on each step, and then he accelerates, leaning into the first turn. Treyvon proudly wears our brown and gold uniforms. He clashes with the blues, yellows, and greens of the other teams in this final race. I quickly pick up the starting block and return to the infield, as the silence from the crowd quickly changes to shouts of encouragement, and eventually a loud roar. The runners come up on the end of the hundred-meter mark.

Standing on the infield with Ray, and Malcolm, we watch as Treyvon pulls ahead to take the lead. Ray stretches out and fires his knees high into the air, anticipating his leg of the race, which will be in a short forty seconds from now.

I give Ray and Malcolm high fives and say, "Let's go, boys. Once in a lifetime."

Ray looks at me and says, "Let's go, Christian. This is our time."

Looking up in the stands, I see my parents and my brother, Little Joe, are sitting with Coach Williams and my girlfriend, Latasha. My father made it out of his job as a mechanic in order to make it from Cleveland down to Columbus with my mom and little brother.

As Treyvon begins the second hundred meters, I can't help but think about my best friend, Terry Witherspoon. Terry died just a month ago, and his death still weighs heavy on our school, on our team, and me. Terry was a senior, just like us. He was the third leg of our relay team. This was supposed to be our year. This was our chance to bring a state championship to East Tech High School.

Terry died on the night of our prom. He had dropped off his date and was heading home.

He shot me a text at one in the morning: What up man?

I texted back: Chillin' with Latasha. You?

Then... nothing. No reply. I figured he just assumed I was busy. No big deal. I would catch up with him on Sunday. Watch the Indians game on TV. Maybe even take a ride down to the stadium. We would sit in the bleachers with the dude who bangs that drum.

It was only a couple hours later that I got the phone call that would change my life forever. My mom told me that Terry was gone.

Dead. My best friend, Terry Witherspoon, was dead.

Just like that, my best friend was gone.

Treyvon holds a narrow lead at the far end of the track.

It didn't take long for the police to determine it was reckless driving that caused the death of my best friend. He went off the road and hit a telephone pole. Just like that, and he was gone. Dead on impact. The worst part was I had sent him a text. A harmless text. I didn't even know he was driving. Was it my fault? The question haunts my brain every minute of every day. Track is usually the place where I can get away from all my problems. It's a time when I can get lost in the moment. But now, in this moment, the thoughts of my best friend consume me.

Treyvon, turns the corner, and sprints the final 100 meters of his first leg. He has dropped back to second place. I can see the strain on his face. The muscles bulging in his legs. He wants to win this race for the team in the worst way. For Terry. For East Tech. His determination fires me up. As a team, we were always fast, but what made us great was our desire to run hard for each other. We pushed ourselves beyond our capacity for each other. It made us see the times we would have never seen running if we only ran for ourselves.

I look at Ray and say, "Let's go, baby. For Terry. Run this race for Terry."

Ray slides onto the track in between the teams from Dayton Dunbar, Cleveland Glenville, and Trotwood-Madison. Four teams, eight bodies cram into the exchange zone as the roar of the crowd pervades the stadium. Ray gets a clean exchange and is off, fitting in between the runners from Dunbar and Glenville, who have a slight lead on the runner from Trotwood-Madison. Already the race is down to four schools. Our chance for a state championship for East Tech hangs in the balance.

Treyvon walks off the track with hands on hips, breathing heavy. I give him a hug and say, "Way to go, T. Way to go."

Treyvon bends over and then falls onto his knees on the infield, and then rolls onto his back, exhausted.

As Ray and the three other runners turn the corner and fly down the backstretch, my mind drifts to Terry's funeral. An entire community gathered in Trinity Cathedral, across the street from Cleveland State University. A large group of students and parents filled the Cathedral and poured out the doors onto the outside steps of the church.

I can still hear the pastor's voice explaining, "Today, Terry Witherspoon is with the Lord." I wrestled with the idea when the pastor said, "All things happen according to God's plan." I wonder how God's plan could possibly be to take away my best friend at the age of eighteen. That doesn't sound like a loving God to me.

At the funeral, Treyvon and Ray and I got up and read notes we had written to Terry after we found out about his death. Treyvon talked about all his best memories on the basketball court with Terry. He told Terry that he would miss him. Treyvon held it together pretty well reading that letter, just like his leg of the race today. He held it together. Ray was another story. He got up and cried like a baby. Saying he would do anything to get Terry back. Anything. Terry's parents sat in the front row. His mom's face was streaked with tears, the pain still fresh in her heart.

When it was my turn, I didn't want to let my best friend down. I wanted to be strong. I told the story about how we ran track together on the Easy Striders summer track team. How we've been running together since we were in middle school. I could feel the tears well up in my eyes. And while I was telling the last story about how we were going to win a state championship in track this year in the name of Terry, the tears rolled down my cheeks.

I didn't bother to wipe them from my face. I missed my friend.

The hardest part was when Terry's father got up and said, "I miss my boy. I miss my son." His body was heaving.

Because we were still on the altar, Ray and Treyvon and I stood behind him. Each one of us put our hands on Mr. Witherspoon. Even today, I can still feel the shake of his body in my hands. I don't know where Mr. Witherspoon got the strength to get up and talk about his son that day, but he said no one should ever have to bury his child. And even though he was filled with an overwhelming sorrow, he told everyone in that church that he will choose to remember the best parts of his son's life, and that we should do the same.

I didn't know if it was possible to become a man in one day, but I felt like I did on the day of Terry's funeral.

When I carried that casket up to the grave on that day in May, something inside of me changed. I had seen a part of the world I should not have yet seen.

Ray holds his own during the first 200 meters of his leg of the race, but around the three hundred mark, he falls farther behind the three other teams. Maybe the emotions of Terry's death were taking effect.

As Ray heads down the backstretch, I look at Malcolm and say, "Just keep it close. Get a good exchange, and we'll have a chance."

Malcolm nods his head, and he slides onto the track into lane four, where Ray has now shifted in order to get a good exchange. Malcolm gets a clean handoff from Ray and files in behind the pack of three other runners. The race is now, without a doubt, down to four teams.

When Ray comes off the track, there are tears in his eyes. I hug my friend. All he says is, "I miss him, Christian. I miss him."

"I know, Ray," I say. "I know."

Malcolm does all he can to keep up with the first three runners. Malcolm is only a sophomore. He has taken the thankless role of replacing Terry on our relay team. Malcolm was our fifth best runner, and he is an unbelievable quarter guy. But he's only a sophomore, not physically as strong as the other runners at this level. I told him just to run his best, keep us close.

Malcolm and I have been struggling with our exchanges. He's not used to the congestion of the other runners in the zone. Sometimes there are six to ten runners jockeying for position. In the district meet, we had a large enough lead that all I had to do was jog and take the baton and cruise to an easy first place victory. Regionals were different. If you jog through the zone, you could lose a lot of time. Malcolm and I bobbled the baton on our exchange, but I was able to get a hold of it, and we took a fourth place at the regional meet, barely qualifying for state.

As Malcolm starts his leg, I think about my future. I have received a full ride to Ohio State on a track scholarship. My girlfriend Latasha has received an academic scholarship to the college of Wooster. The track coach at Wooster said Division III schools do not offer athletic scholarships, but he also said that there are ways to get financial aid. He said he would do all he could to get me in to the school, and find as much money as he could.

Latasha is worried that we'll drift apart. I tried to explain to her that Wooster and Ohio State are only an hour apart. That we'll stay together. Now, with the death of Terry, I feel like I need her more than ever. I can't imagine being away from her. After losing Terry, I can't even begin to imagine what it would be like to lose her as well.

At the 200-meter mark, Malcolm is holding a solid fourth place. This is when he starts his kick. Malcolm surprises everyone with an unbelievable leg. He actually closes the gap between himself and the other runners as they near the backstretch. Maybe he feels he owes it to Terry. By the time the runners reach the last twenty meters of the relay, the runners are bunched up.

It's the situation I feared, a pack of runners coming into the exchange, neck and neck. Malcolm flies into the zone with three other runners, and we all take off. Eight runners slammed together.

"Reach!" he yells.

I throw my arm back.

"Stick!" he yells, slamming the baton into my hand.

And then it happens.

The baton slips from my hand, rotates in the air, and falls onto the track. Tink. Tink. Tink, tink, tink. The baton rattles on the track, as the other runners take off around the first turn.

Running back toward Malcolm, I grab the baton from off the track and sprint after the other three runners, my dreadlocks flapping out to the side.

Already making the turn, the pack is easily thirty meters in front of me. I accelerate into the turn, knowing that any kind of race strategy just went out the window.

I'm in for 400 meters of a full-blown sprint.

Leaning hard into that first turn, I make up some ground. Down the backstretch, I open it up. Full speed.

On that backstretch, I think about what Latasha always says about running. "If you can't run fast for yourself, run fast for your team."

Ignoring the fatigue, I push harder.

Harder.

I think about Treyvon, Ray, and Malcolm. How hard we have worked to make this dream a reality. And then I think about Terry, and how I promised at his funeral to win a state championship.

I think about Coach Williams' words. He told me, "You have all the talent in the world, but you have yet to go to the beyond." He explained that great runners don't just have another gear, they have a fearlessness. They push themselves beyond their regular threshold of pain and ability. He told me that world class athletes go to that place. He said, "You are a great runner, an amazing runner. But you can be elite, world class."

At the two hundred meter mark, I have cut the thirty-meter lead to fifteen meters. And when my legs start to burn, I know that it's time to visit *the beyond*. Kicking it around the turn and into the backstretch, I manage to close the gap to ten meters.

Thinking about what Latasha said about running fast for my team, I dig in deep. Into my heart. My soul.

I think about Terry.

No doubt I love my brother.

The adrenaline pumps through me, and surprisingly, it's not fatigue that I feel, but rather a complete and natural high. My entire focus is on the track and the three runners in front of me.

Even though I'm on Jesse Owens Memorial Track at Ohio State in downtown Columbus, I'm in a completely different place. I'm in the zone. During the last fifty meters, I don't feel anything. I don't hear anything, other than my heartbeat, my life source. As we near the finish line, I slowly close the gap to five meters.

But then, with twenty-five meters to go, my focus begins to fade. And I go to another place. Images of running on the Easy Striders track team with Terry are in my mind. I see him passing me the baton. There is a vision of him playing basketball on the court, driving hard to the basket. Then, out of nowhere, I see his face behind the wheel of his car on the night of our senior prom. The emotions flood over me, and the tears well up in my eyes, blurring my vision. I push myself, harder.

Rage boils inside me.

Mixed with an unexplainable sadness.

Strangely, at the same time, I am at peace with the fact that I cannot change what has happened. I cannot turn back the time.

During the last ten meters of the race, I enter the pack with William Weathers of Trotwood-Madison, Charles Allen of Dayton Dunbar, and Maurice Stone of Cleveland Glenville.

In those last ten meters, I think about time. Track meets are measured in time. Just like life. Life is measured in years, days, hours, minutes and seconds. What if Terry would have texted me a minute later, a second later?

How can the difference in time affect reality? What if my phone was off and I never responded?

What if that telephone pole was ten feet closer or farther down the street?

The "what-ifs" pound my brain.

And then, just as all four runners near the finish line and the yellow tape that spreads across the track, I have this thought: I can't dwell on the past. I can't focus on Terry's death and the things that can't be changed. My life can't be about the "what-ifs." Despite losing my best friend, my focus has to be about moving forward.

I have to pick up the pieces and get on with living my life.

I have to finish strong.

As all four runners lean into the tape for a photo finish, I know in my mind, in my heart, that Terry would have wanted it that way.

🏃 Activities for the short story *Moving Forward*:

1. Writing activity. Write your own ending to this story? Does Christian win the race for East Tech, or does he come in second, third, or fourth? How will the ending that you write change the message that you are trying to send in the story? Write your ending based on what you have read in the story and how the story should end.

_____

_____

_____

_____

_____

_____

_____

_____

_____

_____

_____

_____

_____

_____

_____

_____

Continue on your own notebook paper…

SUMMER

GOLF: THE BACK NINE

"Golfers should not fail to realize that it is a game of great traditions, of high ideals of sportsmanship, one in which a strict adherence to the rules is essential."

—Francis Ouimet
(U.S. Open Champion)

The first nine holes of the junior club championship at Signature of Solon Country Club have me tied with Andrew Ferguson. The stakes are high. The junior club champion gets ten thousand dollars in scholarship money to be used toward college. Andrew and I will both be seniors at Solon High School this year. We both qualified for the finals after a long Saturday of competition. Sunday's competition will determine this year's club champion. Andrew doesn't need the scholarship money for school. For my family, ten thousand dollars in scholarship money would go a long way. Rumor has it that Andrew has already been accepted to Kent State University. There is also another rumor that he has earned a scholarship to play golf there, following in the footsteps of Ben Curtis, who won the British Open. I, Kenny Chan, on the other hand, have not yet been accepted to the college of my choice, nor have I been given a scholarship. However, I do plan on being the first person in my family to go to college.

Another difference between Andrew and me is that Andrew's family lives in the gated community and belongs to the club, and I am allowed to play in the tournament because my dad works here. He is the head greenskeeper. He was hired on originally as general maintenance. Five years later, he was promoted to head greenskeeper. His work ethic is unmatched. My dad is the most honest and hard-working person I know.

As the hot Ohio humidity fills the air, I place my ball on the tee. Hole #10 is a long par 5, over 550 yards with a strip of tall pine trees to the left of the fairway and scattered Oak and Maple trees and a long sand trap on the right. Slowly, I pull back my driver, making sure I keep my eye on the ball and follow through. This is something I have worked on all summer. Coming through the ball, I hit it as hard as I can. The ball takes flight and sails to the left of the fairway, landing at about 230 yards and then rolling another twenty yards, right into the middle of four or five scattered pine trees. They are the best obstacles.

Sliding my driver back in my bag, I watch as Andrew steps up to the tee. He is all of six foot five. Andrew says, "Kenny, I think I saw a woodchuck steal your ball."

My temperature rises. Nothing burns me more than the relentless and sarcastic humor of Andrew Ferguson. He is the number one junior player at Signature, and his arrogance is unmatched. But deep down, I know I can beat him.

After a slow, smooth backswing, Andrew generates enough club speed to crush the ball. It carries 280 yards in the air and rolls another thirty. His drive is easily sixty yards farther than mine and straight down the fairway, which gives him a wide-open shot to the green. With a fairway wood, he'll be on in two. I feel like I'm in a match with Dustin Johnson on the PGA tour.

Meanwhile, I'm stuck back in the pines. I'll have to hit a hooded four iron just to get under the trees and back onto the fairway, and then I'll still be 220 out.

Andrew shoots me a fake smile as he picks up his bag, and we begin our walk toward our second shot. As I walk down the fairway, I consider the fact that today is my chance to show Andrew that I belong on the course with him, and more importantly, earn some money for school. I applied to four different schools: Cleveland State, Youngstown State, Kent State, and the University of Akron. And this summer I have worked harder than ever before in anticipation of this match. Every morning I have been up at 4:30 and to the golf course by 5:00 with my dad. After hitting range balls,

I caddy one loop with two bags, and then I get in 18 holes of my own. Then, I hit more range balls until my blisters form new blisters.

When I get to my ball, Andrew lets out an impatient sigh.

Pulling my four iron from my bag, I line up my shot, take a couple practice swings and punch the ball out from under the pine trees and onto the fairway.

"Looks like your still about 250 out," says Andrew with heavy sarcasm.

"About 220," I say. With hands shaking in anger, I pull my 20-degree hybrid from my bag. Without setting up to the shot, I walk up quickly to the ball and swing as hard as I can, thinking I can knock it on with a full swing from 220. Instead of hitting the ball clean, I lift my head and my entire body. The club catches the top of the ball, and it skims across the fairway grass, until it comes to a stop thirty yards in front of me. Just like Walter Hagan, I mumble every bad word I know under my breath.

"Look out," says Andrew. "Kenny hit a worm burner." Andrew shakes his head, and then he takes his fairway wood out of his bag. He stands behind his ball and takes a couple practice swings. Just like Bobby Jones, Andrew's swing is super smooth. From two hundred and forty yards out, he rockets the ball high into the air. It lands softly on the right side of the green, pin high. "On in two," he says.

I grab my bag and stomp to my ball, which is a convenient and unfortunate thirty yards away. I'm still 190 out, so I keep my hybrid out. This time I take a full swing, and make contact with the ball, the shot I needed last swing. The ball shoots off the face of my club and sails past the green into the bunker behind the green. Everything inside of me wants to break my club over my knee. Taking a deep breath, I collect myself.

When I finally get to my ball, I discover that I'm laying four in the bunker. Correct that, buried in the bunker. I pull my sand wedge from my bag. Taking a couple practice swings, I make sure not to ground my club, a two-stroke penalty. When I hit my shot, it flies past the flag about fifteen feet. I'll be putting for bogey.

"You're *still* away, Kenny," says Andrew, emphasizing the word still.

My putt comes up about three feet short, and I mark my ball.

Andrew lines up his putt, takes a few practice swings. His putt is twelve feet out, has a subtle break, from left to right. He rolls the ball right to the edge of the cup. It seems to rest at the edge of the cup for a long three seconds, and then it drops in, just like Tiger's famous shot at Augusta. "Eagle!" Andrew shouts with a fist pump.

I lip out my three footer and tap in for a triple bogey, eight. With one hole down on the back nine, Andrew is already five strokes ahead of me.

"Ouch," says Andrew. "Should I write you down a snowman."

"Yes," I say, "I got an eight."

Andrew laughs to himself and says, "Too hot for a snowman."

Andrew tees off on #11, a short par four, dogleg right. The only thing that will prevent him from driving the green on this hole is the dogleg. He would have to fly over 150 yards of trees. So he makes the smart play and hits his tee shot two hundred yards, which will give him a straight look to the hole. "Right where I want to be," says Andrew.

Teeing my ball up, I try to remind myself what I need to do. Eye on the ball, small lift of the head to give room for the shoulder to clear and follow through. I do everything correctly, except for the follow through, and my drive slices along the right side of the fairway. Again, I am out of position. I'll have to hit my wedge to get the ball in the fairway. It's official. I'm playing the worst golf of my life, and the worst part is it's when it matters the most.

My second shot winds up about ten feet to the left of Andrew's first shot. "Nice of you to catch up," he says, pulling a wedge from his bag. We are about 120 yards out.

Andrew lands the ball about ten feet above the pin. "I'll be putting for birdie."

If I manage to land my shot on the green, I'll be lucky to putt in for par. My wedge shot lands ten feet from the green.

"Almost," says Andrew. We pick up our bags and walk toward the green.

My chip, somehow rolls close to the cup, and I tap in for a bogey, five.

Andrew's putt just misses the cup, and he taps in for par, increasing his lead by six strokes.

On the way to the next hole, I know I have to figure out how to change the way I am playing. And then I remember to look at the notes I've written on my scorecard. The notes are reminders about why I love to play the game of golf. The first note reads: Bagger Vance.

This note is in reference to my favorite golf movie: *The Legend of Bagger Vance* and a line from the movie that talks about the importance of the grip on your club. I tell myself to relax my grip, and to relax in general. You can't play golf angry.

The #12 hole is a 150-yard par three. The tee box is high on top of the hill, and you have to shoot down to the green below. It's a hole I've played a hundred times.

Andrew hits his next shot on the green, about twenty feet to the right of the pin.

Loosening my grip on the club, I take a nice easy swing. The ball takes flight with a little draw and drops ten feet to the left of the cup.

With a look of complete surprise on his face, Andrew says, "I guess everybody gets lucky once in a while."

Andrew's putt just misses the cup, and he taps in for par.

Finally, I have a chance to gain a stroke. Taking a deep breath, I line up my putt, take a few practice swings and drain it for a ten-foot birdie. Inside, I smile to myself, knowing that I was so nervous on the first couple holes, there was no way I could expect to play the way I knew how. Down five strokes, I have my work cut out for me.

Hole #13 is a 450-yard par four. My drive is a solid two hundred and fifty yards, right in the middle of the fairway.

Andrew steps up to the tee, takes a few practice swings, and crushes the ball. It flies in the air past my ball and then rolls an additional forty yards. 295. Almost 300 yards off the tee, incredible for a high school senior.

Andrew's distance is killing me. My second shot is two hundred to the hole; a full hybrid is what I need to get there. Andrew is looking at 165, an easy seven iron for him.

My second shot flies into the sand trap on the right side of the green, but I've gotten up and down from there before.

Andrew's second shot is, of course, on the green, about eight feet to the left of the pin.

From the sand trap, I hit a shot that rolls within three feet of the cup.

Andrew misses his birdie putt, and we both tap in for par. We are still five strokes apart with five holes to play.

When I get to the tee on #14, I check the notes on my scorecard. The note reads: The Tank!

The Tank is a reference to my favorite golfer on tour, K.J. Choi. K.J. isn't the biggest guy or the farthest hitter on tour, but he is consistent: fairways and greens all day. My message to myself is simple: Play smart and keep the ball in play.

Hole #14 is a long par five. Normally, I would try to kill the ball to keep up with Andrew's big drive. Instead, I take a nice easy swing, and the ball rockets off the face of the driver and carries down the fairway. Even *my* eyes open wide in surprise as the ball lands at

250 yards and rolls another thirty. Two hundred eighty yards is by far the best drive of my life.

Andrew, for the moment is silenced. I can tell he is flustered when he hits his tee shot into a bunch of trees on the left side of the fairway. He slams his driver into the ground and swears to himself.

While Andrew searches for his ball, I line up my second shot. I'm still two hundred and fifty out, but instead of going for the green, I decide to lay-up and trust my short game. My second shot travels a solid two hundred yards, leaving me fifty yards from the green, an easy wedge.

Andrew finds his ball, and somehow manages to punch out onto the fairway. His third shot finds the green. But his shots aren't nearly as crisp as when we started the back nine. Before I pull out my pitching wedge, I check the notes on my scorecard: "It's not about winning. Play for the love of the game!"

A smile spreads on my face. In the midst of playing for that scholarship, I had forgotten about how much I love the game and why I love the game. What I love most about golf is the challenge it presents me. There is nothing I love more than summer mornings on the course, with just a bucket of range balls. Or a twilight round when the sun is going down, and it's just me on the golf course. When I think about those moments, I know, that win or lose today, I'm the luckiest kid on the planet.

With a loose grip on my club, I take an easy back-swing and make perfect contact with the ball. It lands five feet from the pin and sticks on the green. Even though Andrew would never admit it, it seems like he is impressed by this effort. In fact, since the first hole, Andrew's smack talk has diminished to almost nothing.

Andrew's putt comes up two feet short, and then he taps the ball in for a par. I line up my putt, and I see that it breaks two feet from right to left. Setting up to the putt, I take a few practice swings. With a smooth stroke, the ball takes its course toward the hole. Slowly, it begins to break, and at the last second, it catches the back of the cup and falls in for a birdie. I'm down four strokes with four holes to go. But the biggest difference is that my game has gotten more fluid, and now it's Andrew who seems to be gripping his clubs too tight.

My tee shot on a short par four, hole #15, drifts to the right and bounces off the cart path and lands in the middle of some trees. Relief spreads across Andrew's face. He steps up to his ball and crushes his tee shot to within 100 yards of the green.

When I finally find my ball, I try to figure out my best play. My first and most important thought is not to panic. There is a small opening between two trees that leads directly to the flagstick. Lining up my shot, I think to myself, *I can get it through there*. The flight of the ball will have to be perfect. Who did I think I was... The Tank? Taking a smooth backswing, the ball jumps off the face of my nine iron. Instead of flying cleanly through the trees, the ball smacks the side of a tree on the left, but somehow ricochets in the direction of the green. The ball has such velocity that it rolls through the rough and just onto the second cut of the green.

Andrew shakes his head and says, "Are you kidding me, Kenny?"

"Sometimes it's better to be lucky than good," I say, laughing out loud.

Andrew doesn't smile at this. His second shot is filled with anger, and it flies the green by almost thirty feet. He throws his club into his bag. Andrew grabs his wedge and putter and heads to his ball. Andrew will be lucky to make par on this hole. He has a very difficult up and down. And me, with my bank off the tree, I will have a chance at making birdie. I could be down only two strokes going into the final three holes.

Andrew chips onto the green, leaving a long fifteen-foot putt for par.

Before chipping onto the green, I take a few practice swings and notice the slight left to right break. The ball comes off the face of my wedge, and it lands softly, rolling toward the hole. The ball rolls right on target and drops in the hole for a birdie, just like Tom Watson's birdie on the 17th hole at Pebble Beach.

Andrew rolls his eyes in disbelief. Letting out an angry humph, Andrew hurries his putt. He must be feeling the pressure. Striking the ball too hard, it rolls past the cup, leaving him another long putt just to make bogey. Andrew's face has gone from relaxed to super tense. However, he manages to make his eight-foot putt coming back toward the hole, but his lead has diminished to two strokes with three holes to go.

Over the course of the last nine holes, our demeanors have changed. With three holes left, I know that Andrew will have the advantage on #16 and #17, two long par fours, and I will have the advantage on #18, a short par four that goes toward the clubhouse. All I have to do is make up two strokes over the next three holes. I know I can do it.

On the #16 tee, I hit my drive to the left side of the fairway, about one hundred and eighty yards from the green. I purposely hit to the left because on the right side of the fairway is a lake about 270 yards from the tee.

Andrew, on the other hand goes for it. He swings with all he has, but the lake was put there for a reason, a well-placed obstacle. Andrew's tee shot finds the water for a one-stroke penalty. SPLASH. Andrew's second tee shot is the one he should have had first, and his ball lands about one hundred and twenty-five yards from the green.

This is my chance to make up a stroke and go to the last two holes with one stroke to make up for the tie, or maybe two strokes for the win. My second shot comes up just short of the green, but I know I can chip it close and putt in for par.

Andrew hits his next shot onto the green, about fifteen feet from the cup. His once fluid stroke now seems much more uncertain. Andrew's putt looks like it will break four or five times. He steps up to his putt, and somehow, he sinks the putt for a bogey.

Right now, I need a solid chip and good putt to put me one stroke back with two holes to play. My chip shot rolls about three feet short of the cup, and I manage to tap in for par. I have cut the lead to one stroke.

On Hole #17, I outplay Andrew at his own game. After hitting a longer drive and a better iron shot, I stroke a perfect putt for birdie. Andrew makes par to even up the match.

Before I tee up on hole #18, a 320-yard, short par four, I look at the notes on my scorecard. The instructions are simple: Trust yourself.

Feeling confident, I step up to the ball. In my mind, I visualize the shot. Taking a few practice swings, I feel the club in my hand and a smooth stroke. Trusting my swing, I drive my tee shot in a way that would make the Tank proud. It is straight and long, right down the middle of the fairway, leaving me about seventy yards from the green.

Andrew's drive is of course farther, putting him about thirty-five yards from the green.

Even though Andrew's drive is farther, I know that my short game is better. Even though he's closer, I know I can put my second shot close to the pin and put pressure on him to make a great second shot. If I can birdie this hole, I can win.

When I approach my ball for my fairway shot, a few thoughts run through my head. When everybody was sleeping in this summer, I was at the course hitting range balls. When everyone went home early for dinner, I stayed at the driving range or got in one more round of twilight golf. I deserve to win this match. I've earned it.

Setting up to my ball, I think back to all the things I've been thinking about on the last nine holes: Loosen the grip on my club. Be the Tank. Play for the love of the game. Everything feels perfect. I take an easy and smooth backswing, but when I come down on the ball,

I hit it with the hosel of the club. The ball flies to the right of the green and drops right into the bunker. The wind quickly goes out of my sails. But as I work toward my ball, I start to think about what really makes a great golfer. It isn't always about hitting the best shot. It's about having the ability and mental toughness to be able to scramble, to recover, to make the best out of a tough situation. The best golfers are able to overcome bad shots and any other adversity they face on the golf course.

Andrew, to his credit, hits his shot pin high, about twelve feet to the right of the pin. After marking his ball, Andrew says, "Your shot."

I nod my head.

So this is what it all comes down to. One shot, and the opportunity to earn ten thousand dollars in scholarship money, money that would make a big difference to my family. I line up my shot, like I'm playing for the green jacket at the Masters in Augusta. With a clear mind, I take a few practice strokes. And almost in one motion, I touch my club down on the sand, take my backswing and strike the club into the sand, right behind the ball. The ball pops up from the sand, lands safely on the green, and rolls right on course toward the cup. The ball breaks three different times, and I have to catch my breath as the ball drops right in the hole for a birdie.

My first reaction is that I can barely contain myself.

Andrew's eyes widen in disbelief. He will have to sink his putt just to tie.

My second reaction is an awareness of what just happened. It occurs to me that I touched my club in the sand prior to my shot, a two-stroke penalty. However, because I was down in the trap, there was no way that Andrew could have seen it. He would never know.

At first, I don't say anything.

Andrew lines up his putt, takes a few practice swings, and strikes the ball. It rolls toward the hole, and just at the last second, it breaks hard to the left, just missing the hole. He shakes his head and lets out a deep sigh and taps in for a par.

Thinking he has lost, Andrew shakes my hand and says, "Congratulations, Kenny. You played great on the back nine. You deserve to be club champion."

As Andrew utters those words, I know that I do not deserve to be club champion. And I do not deserve that scholarship money. But at the same time, I think about my dad working at the course. I think about how much ten thousand dollars would mean to our family. Ten thousand dollars is almost four months pay for my dad. The money would make a significant difference in our lives, and Andrew would be fine either way. But in my mind, I know that winning this way is wrong. I could never live with myself. My dad's honesty and work ethic stick in my mind. In my heart, I know what is the right thing to do. It's then that I know I have to come clean, before this goes any further.

"Andrew," I say, "on my last shot, I touched my club down in the sand. I get a two-stroke penalty. That would give me a bogey for the hole. You win the match."

Andrew looks at me in disbelief. "You're kidding, right?" he says.

"No, I touched the club in the sand before my shot. A two-stroke penalty gives you the win."

"Are you sure?" Andrew asks again.

"I'm sure," I say. "I can't believe I made such an amateur mistake. I know better. Taking the penalty strokes is the right thing to do."

Winning that scholarship and the club championship was my dream. It was everything I had worked for. But in the back of my mind and in my heart, deep down, I would know that I had not earned it. Without a doubt, I feel proud for telling Andrew the truth.

Andrew shakes his head. "If you think that's the right call," he says.

"I know it is," I tell him.

Walking off the eighteenth green, I tell myself that I will find another way to earn the money that I will need to be the first person in my family to go to college. And I will do it honestly and with integrity.

Questions for *The Back Nine*:

1.   Exercise: The theme of a story is the message that the characters and the story convey to the reader. What is the strongest theme in the story *The Back Nine*? Give one piece of textual evidence for the theme and support your reasoning.

   1.   State one theme of the story:

   _____

   _____

   _____

   _____

   1a.   Textual evidence for the theme:

   _____

   _____

   _____

   _____

   1b.   Explanation of how the textual evidence supports the theme:

   _____

   _____

   _____

   _____

SURFING: BACK ON THE BOARD

"Surfing is the most blissful experience you can have on this planet, a taste of heaven."

—John McCarthy
(Professional Surfer)

It had been almost three months since my best friend died.

It was a shark attack off the black sandy beaches of the Waipio Valley in Hawaii, at our surfing spot. The very same place we've been surfing for ten years, since we were six years old. Misha and I were training for the big Oahu Invitational, which at the time, was a short three months away. Watching Misha catch a wave, I saw the giant head of the Great White shark appear in the wave and take down my best friend and his board. The blood spread through the water like black ink on paper. I was able to get him to shore, but because we live so deep in the Waipio Valley, I wasn't able to get him the medical attention that he needed in time. He died in my arms on the beach. After that, I sat in my room for two weeks without speaking to anyone. For the next month and a half after that, I stopped living. I was a ghost of myself, feeling like nothing was real, and pretending that everything that happened to Misha on the beach that day was only a bad dream.

Almost two months after Misha's death, my father knocked on my bedroom door and said, "Tyler, get your things. We are going to see Mr. Otanka."

Mr. Otanka was a shaman in the Valley and a family friend, but I didn't want to see him or anybody else for that matter. "No," I fired back. "I'm not."

From the other side of my bedroom door, my father said, "You can't continue to live like this. You don't sleep, and you have barely eaten." There was a long pause. My father's voice broke the silence when he said, "Nothing will bring back Misha."

Sitting on my bed, I looked at the picture of Misha and me on my nightstand. We are standing next to each other holding up our surfboards. It was two years ago when Misha took first and I took second place in the fourteen and under division at the Oahu Invitational. He beat me on the last round of competition. Even though he was only fourteen years old at the time, he was easily the best surfer in all the age divisions.

My father knocked on the door again. "Let's go. Get your stuff. Mr. Otanka is waiting."

Misha's death had taken a physical effect on me. I was afraid to look down at my chest because it felt like there was literally a gaping hole where my heart should be. Occasionally, I would put my hands on my chest to make sure it was there because the numbness told another story. Misha's death had caused my own paralysis, like a big wave that keeps you under water for too long.

My father's voice cut through my thoughts. "Otanka is waiting."

Mr. Otanka treated many people in the Valley, and sometimes, people would travel from the heart of the Big Island to be cured. Otanka was known for his herbal cures and spiritual medicine. He did not believe in modern medicine. He believed that true healing came from the earth, and from within. He was my grandfather's best friend, and after my grandfather passed away, he remained friends with my father. Maybe he could help. Besides, what other choice did I have?

I forced myself to get out of bed and walked to the door. Dragging my feet, I followed my dad across our farm. It felt good to feel the fresh air on my face and the earth under my feet.

We climbed into our old Toyota Four Runner and drove a few miles, deeper into the Valley. Mr. Otanka lived in the very center of the Waipio Valley, near the great waterfall. His home was about three miles from our house.

When my father parked the truck outside of Mr. Otanka's house, he looked at me with concern on his face and said, "Mr. Otanka is expecting you. Do you want me to wait until you are finished?"

"No, I'll walk home. It's good to be outside." I slid out of the passenger seat and walked toward the front door of the tiny cabin that sat along a small lake that was formed at the bottom of the waterfall. The lake emptied into a river that ran all the way through the Valley, past our house, and into the ocean. My father backed out of the driveway and drove home.

The view of the waterfall was spectacular. I had to catch my breath. Before walking to Mr. Otanka's cabin, I walked over by the waterfall.

It must be a mile high, I thought to myself, looking up, admiring its beauty and strength. The waterfall crashed into the crystal clear water. I could see all the way to the rocky bottom. As I walked toward Otanka's cabin, I noticed the trees that surrounded the cabin had dark green leaves that seemed to swallow his tiny living quarters. I knocked on the door.

Otanka opened the door. He was my height, thin, but still very fit for his age. He looked at me with his soft brown eyes. He wore a pair of faded green shorts, a plain white T-shirt, and of course, no shoes. Without speaking, he motioned for me to come in. The inside of his cabin was dark and damp. There was some music on in the background, a quiet, meditative music. "Sit down, Tyler," he said.

Moving across the small cabin, I sat in a wicker chair in the corner of the one-room cabin.

"Please excuse the mess," he said, while picking up a few pieces of laundry and throwing them into a basket in the corner. He finally turned to face me and said, "I knew your grandpa."

"I know. My dad says that you were good friends."

When the teakettle began to whistle, he removed it from the stove and poured the hot water into two cups. "Your grandpa was twenty years old when he came to Hawaii in 1970. He left Kent State University after the shootings. Said he had seen enough of the violence in the world." Otanka grabbed two tea bags from the cupboard above the sink. "He came with his girlfriend, Karen. It was a student ambassador program. They took a tour of the Waipio Valley, and they never left. He worked for Mr. Makala for nearly ten years on his taro farm, until Mr. Makala passed away. Mr. Makala left your grandfather the farm in his will. It was on that farm that he raised your father and where you were born."

"I know…" I said impatiently, and then stopped myself, hoping that the tone of my response wasn't rude. Mr. Otanka handed me the cup of tea and sat down in the chair next to me. A strong cinnamon smell filled my nose.

"I know you do, but I want to make a point. Your grandfather was a good man, but all his life, he ran from his pain. He ran from his fears. He internalized everything, and I truly believe that is what cost him his life in the end. It was the fear that killed him. His body could not accept the energy, nor release it in a natural, healthy manner. Soon it caught up with him and took his life. The memory of the death of your friend will do the same to you if you do not come to terms with it." Otanka took a long sip of his tea, and then, he let out a deep breath.

I looked at the deep wrinkles in the dark, leathery skin on his face. "How do I do that?" I asked, shifting uncomfortably in my seat. My chest tightened. "He was my best friend. The pain won't stop."

"I don't doubt that." Otanka gave me a look of compassion and said, "Nothing is more real than death."

"What can I do to ease the pain?" I asked.

He paused for a moment, looked me in the eye and asked, "What is it that you love?"

The question caught me off guard. It seemed completely unrelated to the death of my friend. I gave Mr. Otanka a confused look, as if he had asked the wrong question. "You want to know what I love?" I asked.

Otanka nodded his head and said, "Yes, Tyler. What is it that you love?"

So I thought about his question. I wondered how love could have anything to do with dealing with the sorrow of losing my best friend. But following Otanka's advice, I thought about what I really loved. Many different ideas passed through my mind.

"It's not a difficult question," said Otanka.

After a few minutes of thought, I finally came to this conclusion. "I love my family: my mother, my father, and my older sister. I loved Misha."

"Of course you love your family. And I know you loved Misha. But what is it that you do with your time? What is your true passion?"

I paused for a moment and considered what I loved more than anything. The first thing that came to my mind was the Valley itself. "I love living in the Valley," I said to Otanka, hoping that this was the answer he was looking for.

Otanka stood up from his chair and shook his head from side to side. Raising his voice, and now hovering over me he thundered, "What do you burn for?"

Feeling the pressure of his question and now his physical proximity to me, I searched my brain, thinking. There was one place that I had loved being more than anywhere, but now because of Misha's death, I feared that place. I looked at Otanka and answered, "Being on the water... surfing."

Otanka nodded his head, like this was the answer he was expecting. He said, "You can't run from your past. You can't run from your fears. They will eat you up inside. You must face them head on... You... MUST... get back on the board!"

I dropped my head into my hands and said, "I can't do that, Mr. Otanka. There are too many memories."

Otanka said, "But that is exactly why that is where you must go. Otherwise those memories will haunt you for the rest of your life."

"Forgive me," I said shaking my head, "but I can't do it." I stood up and began walking toward the door of his cabin.

Raising his voice and moving toward me, Otanka said, "Do you want to live like this?" He moved both hands in a downward motion over my slumped body. "For the rest of your life? Is this how you choose to exist?"

I shrugged my shoulders and said, "I don't know what else to do."

"Then you must trust me. You must believe that what I ask you to do will make you better… will heal you."

I considered that for the last two months I had been in shock, and I was in denial that I had lost my best friend. I didn't want to believe it. Part of me truly believed that the next time I went to the beach Misha would be there, surfing, like always. I had played the scenario over and over in my mind. I had come to believe that it would be true. But Otanka was right. I couldn't continue to live like this. He knew I needed help. Looking up, I asked, "What do I have to do to get better?"

The music in the cabin came to an end. Otanka smiled and said, "Follow me."

We walked outside, toward a small shed that was about halfway between the lake and his cabin. We walked to the side of the shed, and standing there was the largest surfboard I had ever seen. It was not a modern board, but one from a long time ago.

He ran his hand along the wood and said, "This was made from the wood of an old Koa tree back in 1912. It was owned by the great Duke Kahanamoku. The wood is heavy, harder to maneuver. It will make you stronger." He turned the board over and pointed to the single fin on the bottom of the board. "Some of the early boards had no fins or maybe only one. As you know, the newer boards have two or three fins to help with the navigation of the board. This board is twelve feet long and weighs over 70 pounds. If you can control this board, you can control anything. Including your mind." Otanka had a look of complete satisfaction on his face.

I held my hands up, as if to put a stop to all of it. "That board is too big for me," I said.

Otanka just smiled and said, "You must trust me. I will see you on the beach tomorrow morning. When the sun comes up, we will begin our training."

I turned to walk away.

"Aren't you forgetting something?" he asked.

I turned and faced Otanka and asked, "What?"

Effortlessly, he picked up the board and handed it to me. "You will need this," he said with a wink. Walking back toward his cabin, Otanka said over his shoulder, "Chop wood, carry water."

Without understanding what Otanka was talking about, I lifted the oversized board. Even though it felt heavy in my hands, I could feel an energy coming off the board, a force of some kind. Struggling with its weight, I positioned it below my armpit as I began the walk back to my house, wishing that I had asked my father to stay with the Four Runner.

On the walk back to my house, I thought about Misha and all the good times we had surfing together, working together, playing together. Even though he was my neighbor and lived next door, we were like brothers. My heart felt the pain for the loss of my best friend, but at the same time, because of the weight of the board and its awkward shape and size, I was forced to stop thinking about Misha and had to refocus my attention to the board. I would shift the board from one arm to the other. Then I would hoist it over my head or carry it on my back. The walk back to my family's taro farm seemed to last an eternity.

When I finally got home, I walked directly to the barn and stood the board up against it. Then, I grabbed my bucket and headed to the farm and began to pull the taro roots from the wet ground. It was the first time since Misha's death that I had worked. The thoughts of Misha's death flooded my head. The image of the shadow of the shark in the wave was burned into my mind. Every part of me wished that it were me on that wave and not Misha. The guilt in me was stronger than ever. In my mind, I decided that Misha's death was my fault. If I had been on that wave, it would have been me. If the timing were different in any way, Misha would still be here. Misha wanted to surf the Pipeline at Oahu that day, but I insisted on staying close to home. I would do anything to have that day back, to live it differently. It was my decision to stay in the Valley that day that caused Misha's death. In many ways, and for many reasons, I didn't feel like I was worthy of living. I wanted to die.

As I pulled root after root, anger flooded my veins, there was a heavy sagging in my chest, and then the sensation would return, as if there was a hole seared through my heart, and then I would be numb. The day of Misha's funeral I destroyed all the surfing trophies in my room and punched my wall until my knuckles bled. I was enveloped in loneliness because I was consumed by the realization that I could no longer call my best friend and hear his voice on the other end of the line. The only thing I could do now was read old emails and text messages and play back old voice messages from my friend. This reality was difficult to digest.

After two solid hours of work, my father came outside. He didn't say anything. He simply started working next to me, and for some reason, that was exactly the right comfort that I needed.

Realizing how lucky I was to have a family who loved me so much brought me a much-needed peace. And the beauty of that thought filled me with a happy kind of sadness. And out on the field, farming the taro, for the first time since Misha died, the tears rolled frankly down my cheeks. The pain came from way down deep in my heart. The tears actually made me feel a sense of relief. Maybe I was beginning to heal. Of course, I made sure to position myself so my father did not see the tears.

My father killed one of our chickens that night, and after cleaning the chicken, he wrapped the meat up in the leaves of the taro plant. We cooked it over an open fire. My mom and sister joined us for poi and chicken. It was the first full meal I could stomach in two months. After dinner, from the window of my room, I could hear my father quietly playing his ukulele by the fire. The music made me breathe and relax. It felt like the first time I had actually taken a deep breath since I lost my best friend. That night was also the first night I had really slept since Misha died. It was a good thing because I was going to need the energy.

My alarm went off at 5:30 the next morning. It would give me enough time to get the board and carry it the mile and a half to the beach where I would meet Mr. Otanka. Before I left Otanka's house the day before, he specifically told me to carry the board to the beach each day. He said, "Chop wood, carry water."

I would have to ask him what he meant by that.

When I arrived at the beach, Otanka was already sitting Yoga style, facing out toward the ocean. Even though it was a chilly morning, he was wearing only his shorts and a T-shirt. When I was about ten feet from Mr. Otanka he turned and said, "Tyler, good for you for being here on time. Let's get started. Have a seat next to me."

Confused, I faced Otanka and said, "I thought you were going to help me with my surfing?"

Otanka smiled. "Before you can control your board, you must be able to control your mind."

Shaking my head, I asked, "Who are you? The Dali Llama?"

He winked at me, and tapping his head, he said, "Otanka much smarter."

Tilting my head, I asked, "Mr. Miagi?"

He flexed his biceps. "Much stronger."

"Jackie Chan?" I asked, playing along.

He nodded his head and without missing a beat, he said, "Otanka is much better looking."

The laughter came from both of us. It felt strange to the muscles of my face because it seemed like forever since I had used those muscles to laugh or even smile.

"Sit next to me," he said. "Like this." He showed me a sitting position, legs crossed, hands gently resting on his knees. "Follow your breath through your nose, through your head, into your lungs, your belly, down your legs and into your feet. Follow it back through your body and then breathe it out into the ocean air. Think positive energy in; negative energy out."

I tried the breathing technique. Looking out at the ocean, I questioned being on the beach at six in the morning with Mr. Otanka. I understood being at the beach to surf, but being there to practice my breathing did not make any sense to me.

As if he could hear my thoughts, in a stern voice Otanka commanded, "Close your eyes. You must focus on your breath. All thoughts must pass like the river."

When I closed my eyes, the first image I saw was Misha on his bright yellow board, and then I saw the shadow of the shark in the wave. Then, all I could see was red: Misha's blood. I could not erase these thoughts from my mind. I could see Misha's dark red blood contrasting with the sandy beaches of the Valley. Each time, I did my best to let them pass on by, but each time, the horrible images of blood-soaked sand dominated my mind.

Over and over, Otanka would tap my leg and say, "The river."

Imagining a river, I did my best to let each image, each thought, drift past me. I chose to think of the waterfall by Otanka's house, and the river that ran past our house, and into the ocean. Slowly, the images and thoughts stayed for shorter and shorter periods of time. I followed my breath the way Otanka had instructed me, and with each breath, I could feel my body begin to slow down, to relax. The sand sifted through my fingers.

After what seemed like five minutes, Otanka's voice interrupted my meditation. "You have been sitting for almost an hour. Even though it might not seem like it, you have done some important work. You are starting to heal."

I looked at Otanka skeptically. I didn't feel like I was healing.

Otanka handed me the board and said, "Start by the sandbar and work your way toward the larger waves. The larger board will take some getting used to." He stopped and looked at me and said, "I know you are afraid to get into the water, but you must do this. Without hesitation. With a clear mind."

Reluctantly, I grabbed the surfboard and waded into the shallow water, the waves crashing against my knees. Body shaking, from the cold, from the fear, I slid onto the board and began to paddle out toward the sandbar. Each time I saw the water change color, I imagined it was a shark, *the* shark, Misha's shark, and I yearned to turn back.

The giant board was almost twice as long as my Billabong board and getting through the water was far more difficult. Yet there was something about the board, something about the energy that seemed to give me a renewed sense of confidence. Soon, I was far enough out, and a set of waves was coming in. Paddling fast, I was soon caught up in the current of the wave, then quickly on my feet, and the board settled in. The size of the board made it difficult to maneuver. I lost my balance and crashed into the water.

Again and again, I paddled out and made myself ride the board toward shore, and each time, I came crashing down. It wasn't until the fifteenth try that I was able to maintain my balance and ride the wave up to the shore. By then, the fatigue had set in. The muscles in my legs burned. I wanted to quit. I picked up the board and headed toward Otanka, thinking that this was enough for my first day.

But when I was close to the beach, Otanka called out, "Attack the wave! Be more aggressive! Don't settle for less than your best effort!"

"But I am tired!" I shouted above the roar of the surf.

Either Otanka did not hear me, or he pretended not to hear. He simply pointed me back toward the ocean.

Redirecting myself, I headed back into the water, and I paddled back out to catch the next wave. Each set of waves got higher and higher, from five to eight feet by the sandbar to eight to ten feet farther out.

Each time when I got close to the beach, Otanka barked instructions. "Stay lower! Use more of your lower body! Focus on your technique! Focus on your breath!"

I did my best to follow his directions.

After each attempt, he would say, "This time breathe from your heart! Now, breathe from your belly! Make it burn!"

Even though I was exhausted, listening to the instructions of Otanka made me forget about everything except fulfilling his commands.

Otanka called me over after I rode one last wave toward the shore. "We will meet here at the same time everyday for the next three weeks," he said matter-of-factly. "Rain or shine. You, me, and the board. Without fail."

"Yes, sir," I managed to say.

"The rest of the day, while you farm the taro and make the poi, focus on your breath. When the bad thoughts come, let them drift down the river." Then he smiled, motioned toward the board and said, "Carry the board back home." He laughed to himself. "Chop wood, carry water."

I think I was starting to understand what he meant.

For the next three weeks, I met Mr. Otanka on the sandy beaches. Each day was the same routine. One hour on the beach, in meditation. I released my thoughts, while grabbing the gritty sand and letting it sift back onto the beach like Otanka's waterfall. When the thoughts came, I did my best to release them down the river.

The meditation sessions were followed by more intense training on the long board. Some days brought beautiful Waipio sunrises and others were filled with heavy rain. No matter the weather, I practiced with Otanka.

My strength improved significantly, and my ability to control the board became greater. My confidence grew and grew, and slowly, very slowly, my fears subsided. After two weeks on the big board, I was allowed to surf on my own board. After working on the long board, I was surfing on my shorter board better than ever. My turns were sharper, and I felt like I had more control on my board. By the end of the third week of training with Otanka, my confidence was high.

Thoughts of Misha and the shark settled, like gravel to the bottom of a clear pond, not unlike the one that was next to Otanka's cabin. The meditation and the focus that was required to surf on the big board had retrained my mind.

On the last day of the third week, I said, "Mr. Otanka?"

"Yes, Tyler. What's on your mind?"

"On the day Misha died, he wanted to surf the Pipeline at Oahu to prepare for the Invitational. I told him it was too far away and that we should just practice here in the Valley." I let out a deep breath. "If we had gone to Oahu, Misha would still be here. His death is my fault."

Otanka shook his head. "You did not kill your friend."

Shaking my head, I said, "We wouldn't have been here if I had listened to him."

Otanka looked out over the ocean and said, "It is written."

"What do you mean?" I asked.

"You cannot change the past. What's done is done. You must accept that which cannot be changed."

Looking at Otanka I said, "I never even had a chance to say goodbye."

With that, Otanka's eyes widened, and he said, "Ah, I think we are ready."

"Ready for what?" I asked.

"To go see Misha."

Confused, I looked at Otanka.

"It is time to say goodbye." Otanka motioned to the sand, indicating that I should sit down. "Begin your meditation."

Quietly, I followed Otanka's instructions. Sitting Yoga style, I began to breathe deeply, and because I had been practicing every day for the last three weeks, I was quickly into my meditation.

Otanka's voice came softly. "Remember Misha in a happy moment, where there was happiness and laughter."

I searched my brain for all the good times that I shared with Misha, and the one time that stood out was when Misha and I got lost in the Valley when we were little. We had gone on a hike, and we didn't think we could find the way back to our houses. I began to cry, but Misha put his arm around me like a big brother and said, "Have no fear. Misha is here." I told him he sounded like a superhero and that made us both laugh. We ate our sandwiches that we had packed for our hike, and by the time we were finished eating and telling stories, his father had found us. We were barely a half-mile from our houses.

Otanka's voice came again. "Have you thought of a moment?"

"Yes," I said, nodding my head, picturing the scene in my mind as clearly as if it had happened yesterday.

Otanka said, "Feel the happiness of that moment. No one can take away your memories of your best friend. They will stay with you forever. Misha's energy will be with you... forever."

I could feel the tears begin to well up in my eyes.

"Now, say goodbye to your friend. The way you wish you could have."

I imagined Misha and me both as old men, standing on the beach, with our families, a lifetime of friendship together, raising our families together. Having gone to the University of Hawaii together. In that instant, I saw a lifetime with my friend. In my mind, I gave him a long hug and told him that he was my best friend and that I loved him.

After a few more minutes, Otanka's voice came again. "Accept all emotions, take all positive energy from Misha. And say goodbye."

I took Misha's smile, his constant optimism, his passion for surfing, and the love he had for life. I took all those things and imagined holding them in the palms of my hands, and then I moved them in to the empty place in my heart... the place that I was afraid to look down at for the fear that there was nothing there. The tears rolled down like the Waipio waterfall. But somehow, now, the tears were different. A peace came over my entire body. I heard Otanka singing a powerful song. Looking up, I saw him standing with his arms spread open, facing the rising sun.

When he finished, I asked, "What were you singing?"

"A song. I was asking the mother earth to hold and protect you." He smiled and said, "We are done for the day."

As I began to walk away, he said, "Same time tomorrow. Bring your own board."

The next day, Otanka was waiting for me at the beach. He pointed to an old fisherman on his boat rocking on the water. Otanka said, "We are going to the North Shore of Oahu. It is time to surf the Pipeline."

"I don't know…" I began to say.

Without allowing me to finish, Otanka walked into the water and waded out to the boat and climbed on board.

Reluctantly, I followed.

When I finally got in the boat, Otanka said, "This is Mr. Bagoli. He has been fishing these waters for sixty years."

"Good morning," I said.

Mr. Bagoli nodded and put the boat in gear, and we were off. The old boat bucked over the waves as we cruised toward the waves of the North Shore.

"My friend here is going to surf the Pipeline," Otanka said to Mr. Bagoli.

"Looking to catch the perfect wave?" he asked.

"Something like that," said Otanka.

Otanka talked loudly over the roar of the engine. "Surfing is a lot like fishing. You must see the perfect catch… much like riding the perfect wave. Imagine it, see it in your mind's eye, and it will be."

"What do you mean?" I asked.

"Visualization. See it before doing it. Believing," Otanka said. Then he continued, "The other part is courage. The great fisherman Santiago needed courage to survive. It will be a while until we get to the North Shore. From now until we get there, I want you to imagine yourself riding the perfect wave, each movement, being in the tube. See it, hear it, feel it. Without fear, without reservation."

I looked to Otanka, who merely nodded his head.

During the ride, I imagined myself catching that wave, getting in the tube, seeing the wave break just right, feeling every turn, and hearing the waves crash around me.

At the North Shore, we anchored off to the side of the giant waves that towered over us and came crashing down. Otanka suggested starting small and working my way up. Paddling out into the unpredictable ocean, all I could think about was Misha and the shark. But quickly, as these thoughts entered my head, I remembered my training, and I would let each thought drift past, down the river.

The waves at the North Shore were much bigger than the waves in the Valley. However, I would soon discover that my training on Otanka's big board would make all the difference. It had given me significantly more strength. I had more control and could make sharper turns, even on the bigger waves. Plus, I had another strength, the memory of my friend. After surfing the smaller waves for about an hour, Otanka said it was time to get into the Pipeline, surf the biggest.

I took about ten runs. After each try, I became more and more comfortable. The last run I took was on a twelve-foot wave. It was the wave I had imagined on Mr. Bagoli's boat. I paddled hard and stood up at the crest of the wave. Picking my line, I settled into the wave, and it embraced me and broke just right. Images of the shark shot through my head. Images of Misha flashed in like a slide show. But then like the river, I let them float on by. Gliding on the water, my hand touching the wave, I experienced something I had never felt before. It was pure peace, a oneness with the wave, to the point where I didn't know where my body left off and the wave began. From the waterfall, to the river, to the quiet pond outside Otanka's cabin. Complete silence. Complete acceptance. The wave... and me... were one.

As the wave flattened out, I allowed myself to drop into the water. It felt good on my skin. Swimming toward the shore, I could see Otanka smiling.

At the shore, Otanka said, "Well done, Tyler. You have come far."

"Mr. Otanka," I said, "thank you for helping me."

"You are welcome," Otanka said, "but your healing has just begun. It will still take some time."

Picking up my board, I said, "Misha died when we were training for the Oahu Invitational. The competition is a week away. Would it be wrong to compete in the Invitational? Would it be disrespectful to Misha?"

Otanka looked to be pondering the question. "Are you asking me if your best friend would want you to continue to live your life, even though he is gone?"

"I guess that's the question."

Otanka took my hand and pulled me in for a hug. With the waves crashing against the shore, Otanka said in my ear, "Over the last few weeks your heart has grown. Your mind has grown. Your spirit has grown. There is nothing you cannot do." Then Otanka smiled. "Surfing in the competition, living your life, this is the best honor you can give to your friend."

Questions on *Back on the Board*:

1. Symbolism is when an object or person represents more than what it is? In the short story *Back on the Board*, Otanka gives a large surfboard to Tyler. The board once belonged to the great Duke Kahanamoku. What does the surfboard represent in the story?

_____

_____

_____

_____

_____

_____

_____

_____

1a. Textual evidence example #1:

_____

_____

_____

_____

_____

_____

1b. Explanation of how the textual evidence supports
the symbolism:

_____

_____

_____

_____

_____

_____

_____

_____

2. Can you give another example of symbolism from
the story?

_____

_____

_____

_____

_____

_____

_____

_____

_____

_____

_____

OVERTIME

BOXING: FIGHTING BACK

"When you get tired of getting knocked down and want to pack it all up, don't. Just brush yourself off and keep on going, because the fight is not over until the final bell."

—Joe Frazier
(Professional Boxer)

I jam the clutch into first gear as my black, rusted-out Honda Civic jumps forward and stalls for the third time on the way to school. Not even my car is on my side. I just got my license a couple months ago, and I feel like I'm still learning how to drive stick. The Civic is ten years old and has close to 200,000 miles on it, but my dad says these cars last forever. Unfortunately, for me, he's correct. The driver in the car behind me lays on his horn as I frantically try to twist the key to get it started again.

A boy leans out the window and yells from the passenger seat from the car behind me, "Let's go, Loser!"

Looking into my rearview mirror, I see Danny Amato and his best friend Joey Liston. Danny lays on the horn again.

My blood begins to boil, and at the same moment, my hands begin to shake. It's the perfect mixture of anger and fear.

Finally, the car starts, and I slide the clutch into first gear. The car lunges forward, and I'm off. I coast through the school zone and pull into the student parking lot, with Danny and Joey attached to my bumper.

After pulling into my parking spot, Danny pulls in right next to me. It's the last regular day of school before finals, and all I want to do is go through a day where I don't have to put up with their constant harassment, face their torment.

Putting the car in neutral, I pull back on the parking break and remove the key. Grabbing my backpack from the passenger seat, I open the driver side door.

As I push my door open, Danny pulls it open at the same time. When I stand up, we are face to chest. Danny is almost a foot taller than me, plus he has me by about fifty pounds. Because he is so close to me, I can smell his cheap aftershave as he jams his finger in my chest. "Hey, Samantha. Your driving sucks," he says.

Narrowing my eyes, the anger shoots through my entire body. I clench my fists and begin to shake. My name is Sam, but Danny thinks calling me Samantha is hilarious. It's what entertains him.

"I should kick your ass right here," he says, staring into my eyes. His eyes are tiny black holes that match his jet-black hair.

I shrug my shoulders. His wanting to kick my ass is nothing new. Danny's taunting is relentless. Today is no different than yesterday or the day before that. Besides, he has Joey to impress.

Danny raises his fist and starts to throw a punch to my face. I duck my head and wince, expecting the blow. It wouldn't be the first time he jacked me in the face. Maybe he doesn't deliver the punch because there isn't a sufficient audience in the parking lot.

When I open my eyes, Danny laughs and smiles to himself.

He grabs my backpack and yanks it off my shoulder, unzips it, and turns it upside down, emptying the contents of the bag all over the parking lot. Of course it's a windy day, and the papers take off in different directions.

"You better get your homework, Dork," Joey says, while stepping on one of the sheets of paper and twisting his foot, grinding it into the asphalt.

Danny finishes shaking the backpack and tosses it on the ground. "Yeah, and you better hurry up. Homeroom starts in five minutes."

They both head into the building, laughing. They leave me to gather up about fifteen sheets of homework, notes, and my final paper for English class.

In the building, I try my locker combination for the fifteenth time, and still, it doesn't open. By the time the janitor opens it with a locker key, I am ten minutes late to my first period class, Pre-Calc.

Mr. Jacobs doesn't say anything to me. He doesn't ask, "Is everything okay? Or, why are you late?" Instead, he rolls his eyes and hands me a pink detention slip, and without missing a beat, he proceeds to show the class how to solve the problem on the board, our last review before tomorrow's final exam.

Sliding into my seat in the back of the room, I let out a deep sigh and open my notebook to copy down the problem. The entire time during class I consider the fact that it's the end of my sophomore year, and I come to the conclusion that there's no way I'm going to be able to withstand two more years of Danny's incessant bullying.

Unfortunately, there are a couple problems with this idea:

1. My family isn't planning on moving any time soon.
2. Danny is significantly bigger and stronger than I am.

After school, I sit in detention and listen to the second hand tick the seconds off the clock. The girl next to me with blonde hair, a bright blue top, and a black mini-skirt is popping her gum, and she smells like watermelon. Her name is Sarah Stevenson. I've seen her around school, and I've actually thought about asking her out, but she doesn't even seem to recognize the fact that I'm sitting right next to her. Sitting in the back of the room, I consider that my dating life is nonexistent, and that not many things in my life seem to be going my way. Despite trying to figure out a way to fix it, I can't seem to find an answer. Fortunately for me, the agonizing and seemingly eternal forty-five minute detention comes to an end. I get up from my seat and leave the room without Sarah even noticing.

When I get to the parking lot, I can see banana smeared all over the handle of my car. Just enough of a pain, and they can't really get in trouble for it. I open the back door and climb from the back seat into the front seat. On the drive home, I think of ways to get back at Danny and Joey. I consider every cowardly way there is: slashing tires, egging or toilet papering their houses. But these acts of retribution will just stir up even more punishment. I have to figure out a way to not only get back at them, but to stop them. Whatever I do… it has to be just humiliating enough.

When I get home, my dad is just pulling in the driveway from his job as a CPA. That's a Certified Public Accountant, a bean counter. Things have been much less stressful since tax season has ended. My dad wears a beige suit, a white button down shirt, and a solid red tie. He is tall and skinny. I guess skinny runs in the family, and I'm still waiting for the tall.

"Sam, how was school today?" he asks, parting his brown hair to the side.

"Another day full of fun and learning," I mumble with mock excitement.

"What's that supposed to mean?" my dad asks, pushing his glasses up on his nose.

"It was fine," I say, turning away from my dad and heading up the driveway.

"Hey, what's going on? What's the matter?" my dad asks, trying to catch up with me.

"It's a long story?" I say, avoiding him and walking toward the house.

He grabs onto my shoulder and stops me in my tracks. "Hey, this is your dad you're talking to. What's going on?"

I turn and look at my dad. In my mind, I think about the fact that Danny has been picking on me since eighth grade, and I haven't ever brought the subject up. For three long years, I've just been taking it. I'm not sure what makes me divulge all that's been going on, all that's been pent up inside me for so long. I guess everyone has a tipping point. Knowing my dad has no idea about the complexity of the situation, I throw it out there, just to see what happens. "Can you help me get back at Danny Amato?"

My dad takes a step back. "The kid from school?" He taps his finger on his head. "Why do you need to get back at him?"

Looking down at the ground, I say, "He won't leave me alone. Every day it's something."

Taking off his glasses, my dad rubs his eyes. He does this whenever he's thinking hard about something. "Have you told the principal?"

I shake my head. "That's not how things work."

"So you're being bullied?" he asks, trying to get a good look at my face.

"Pretty much."

"I see," my dad says, nodding his head. "For how long?"

"For about three years..." After opening a can of worms, I try to backpedal. I say, "You know what, Dad. It's no big deal. I'll figure it out."

My dad's voice stops me. "Three years?" he says. "And you haven't said anything?" He lets out a deep breath and scratches his head, pacing back and forth on the driveway. After a long silence, he says, "You know what? I have an idea."

"What's that?" I ask, turning to face my dad.

"I know a guy who might be able to help you. There comes a time when you just have to stand up for yourself." He starts walking back down the driveway toward his Jeep and says, "C'mon, let's go for a ride."

"Where are we going?" I ask.

He waves me over to his Jeep Wrangler and says, "I have a friend you might want to meet."

My dad drives the Jeep down the road and calls out over the wind. "I do some accounting for a landscaper I know. He was also a golden gloves boxer. Then he opened his own landscaping business. I think he might be able to help you."

"Why would he help me?" I ask.

"He's a good man and one hell of a fighter," my dad says, smiling.

"I don't know anything about boxing," I say.

"That's why you are going to learn."

I take a deep breath and swallow hard. "I don't think this is such a good idea."

My dad gets a stern look on his face and asks, "What's your alternative? You want things to continue the way they are?"

As we get off the exit that leads into downtown Youngstown, I think about those two questions. My alternative is to continue to face the bullying, and no, I didn't want to keep facing Danny and Joey. A few traffic lights later, we pull into a shop entrance.

We get out of the Jeep and walk to the front door of the shop. My dad knocks on the door, and a man slowly pulls the door open. He is wearing dark blue pants and a light blue shirt with patches of dirt. The shirt reads: Sanchez Landscaping. His expression quickly turns into a smile when he sees my dad. The man is about five feet ten inches tall. He is solid, sturdy.

"John, how are you?" he asks with a strong accent, while extending his hand.

My dad shakes his hand and says, "Doing just fine. I'm here with my son, Sam. Sam, this is Carlos Sanchez, *The Middleweight Golden Gloves Champion.*" My dad says *The Middleweight Golden Gloves Champion* like he's a ringside announcer.

Carlos shakes my hand. His hand feels like sandpaper, and his handshake crushes my hand. "What can I do for you?" he asks.

"My son is having some trouble at school. He needs to learn how to defend himself."

Carlos nods his head knowingly. He pauses for a long minute, looking me up and down. He turns to my father and says, "I'm kinda out of the fight business."

"I see," says my dad. "What if I paid you for the lessons?"

Carlos brings his lips tightly together. He pauses for a moment and then says, "It's not about the money."

"I understand that," my dad says. He looks at the shop in front of him, and then, my dad's face lights up.

He says, "I have an idea. What if Sam worked here this summer? He could work for the lessons."

Carlos scratches his head, his face filled with uncertainty. "Uh, I don't know." He looks me up and down, again, sizing me up, maybe wondering if I could handle the work. But then something in his body language changes, and after a long pause, he says, "I'll tell you what. Maybe we could make some kind of deal. I'm a little short-handed here at the shop. Sam can work here this summer. And while he's working, I'll train him."

"You mean like a kind of trade?" my dad asks.

"Yeah, like a kind of trade. Of course, I'll pay him as well. I'll just deduct from his paycheck for the lessons."

Looking over at me, my dad asks, "You okay with that?"

My initial apprehension has left me, and now Carlos's suggestion brings the excitement inside of me to an all-time high. All I can think about is getting revenge against Danny and Joey. Without even thinking about it, the word "Yes" comes flying out of my mouth.

Carlos exposes a big toothy grin and says, "All right then, it's a deal. Can you start tomorrow?" he asks.

"I have final exams at school the next three days. Can I start on Saturday?"

Carlos nods his head. "Saturday it is." He puts out his hand, and gives me another hand-crushing handshake.

My dad looks at Carlos, smiles, and says, "I owe you one."

The next few days I go to school to take my final exams, and because of the testing schedule, I am able to carefully avoid Danny and Joey.

When Saturday morning rolls around, I drive to Carlos's garage, wearing a T-shirt, jeans, and a brand new pair of tan work boots that my dad bought me from Sears.

At the shop, I am given a quick tour. Behind the shop, Carlos has all of his trucks parked. There are giant bags of mulch, fertilizer, and grass seed. In his garage, he has just about every tool I could ever imagine. He has rakes, chainsaws, wheelbarrows, long-handle shovels, spades, and pitchforks, all hanging from hooks.

After the quick tour, he introduces me to his crew of workers. First, there is a giant guy named Tommy. He is well over six feet tall with bulging biceps that are exposed by his sleeveless T-shirt. Then there is Nate, who is bald and has a good-sized belly. In fact, everything about Nate is round. And finally there is Alvin, who is about my height and my size. But I can see that he is wiry strong. The introductions are brief, because then, the work begins.

At the shop at seven in the morning, we load tools on top of an already full two-ton dump truck. Carlos explains to me that the truck is full of brown, double-shredded mulch. We toss rakes and pitchforks on top of the mulch. Tommy easily hoists two wheelbarrows on top of the mulch like they're made out of light plastic. Alvin and Tommy get in a pickup truck and sit next to Nate, who starts up the truck.

Carlos calls to me from the driver seat of the two-ton. "C'mon. Jump in," he says.

I step up into the passenger seat, and Carlos puts the monstrous truck into gear. The truck rumbles to life, and we are on our way. I am both nervous and excited because I am on my way to my first real job experience. I don't know what to expect.

Over the roar of the engine, Carlos explains, "We have about fifteen yards of mulch to spread at a banquet hall. We planted a bunch of plants there this week, so it will take most of the day to put the mulch down." We bounce around in the truck. "I'll have you doing mostly wheelbarrow work today, and just about whatever side jobs we need done."

"Sounds good," I say.

After fifteen minutes in the truck, we pull up to Brookhaven Banquet Hall. I jump down from the truck and stand to the side, as Alvin, Tommy, and Nate spring into action. Tommy lowers the gate of the two-ton, and Alvin climbs up into the bed of the truck on top of the mulch. He hands down the two wheelbarrows and the rakes.

Carlos says, "Tommy and Sam will wheel the mulch. Sam will bring it to me, and Tommy will bring it to Nate. Alvin will load the wheelbarrows, and Nate and I will spread the mulch."

Without any discussion, the work begins. Alvin slides the mulch from the back of the truck into my wheelbarrow. I lift up the heavy load and quickly discover it is heavier than what I expected, but I don't want to embarrass myself. Struggling to balance the weight of the mulch, I spill a good amount in the parking lot, but somehow, I manage to make it over to Carlos.

"Dump it right here," he says.

Lifting the handles of the wheelbarrow, I dump the mulch in an open area, and Carlos begins to spread the mulch.

While heading back to the truck for more mulch, I think to myself, *At this rate, I'll never make it through the day*.

And to make matters worse, the summer sun begins to peak out from the morning fog.

Alvin pitches mounds of the dark-brown, double-shredded mulch into my wheelbarrow. While Alvin loads my wheelbarrow, he makes fun of my brand new boots and how they stick out like a sore thumb.

Tommy works like a dog, and he seems to get two loads of mulch for every one that I struggle to get to Carlos.

Soon, the morning fog has completely burned off, and the sun sits high in the summer sky. The back of my neck starts to burn. The muscles in my shoulders are on fire, and my new boots have created painful blisters on the backs of my feet.

By the time lunchtime rolls around, I am exhausted.

Pulling out my brown bag, I grab my peanut butter and jelly sandwich. We sit in the shade of an old oak tree just in front of the banquet hall.

Carlos asks, "How you doin' so far, Sam?"

"Hanging in there," I say. From under the oak tree, I can see that the truck is just under half full. We have moved and spread about ten yards of mulch in three hours.

"We should knock the rest of this out this afternoon, and be done by three. I like to send my guys home early on Saturday."

Early? I think to myself, feeling like I've already worked a full day.

Too soon, lunch is over, and we are back at it. The sun continues to beat down mercilessly, but I find myself working harder, just to get the rest of the mulch out of the back of that dump truck. I am amazed by the pace and the hustle of both Tommy and Alvin. Nate is also a good worker, and Carlos is right there in the dirt with us, even though he is the owner of the company.

When three o'clock rolls around, the Brookhaven Banquet Hall looks like a completely different place. The mulch has brought out the colors of the plants that were planted during the week. The orange and yellow colors pop out from the mulch.

Carlos smiles and says, "Good work, fellas. Let's pack it up and head back to the shop."

Tommy spins the wheelbarrow around and hoists it up into the back of the two-ton. He picks it up like it's a feather. Then he looks at me and says, "You try."

Following Tommy's technique, I spin the wheelbarrow around, grab the metal bars on the bottom, and I barely manage to slide the wheelbarrow up to Alvin.

Alvin grabs the end of it and pulls it onto the bed of the truck. He gives me a wink. "Good work, newbie," he says.

I ride with Carlos back to the shop. As we pull out of the parking lot, Carlos says, "Do you know what I love about landscaping?"

"Feeling sore and exhausted?" I say.

Carlos laughs at this. "The sense of satisfaction. When we got to that banquet hall at the beginning of the week, Brookhaven didn't look anything like it does now. We put down fifteen yards of mulch, and we planted twenty trees, sixty shrubs, and three hundred plants. My work gives me a tremendous amount of satisfaction."

"Do you always work with your crew?" I ask.

"Sometimes. It just depends on the day. I knew you were going to be working today, and I wanted to make sure things worked out on your first day. Plus, I want my guys to know that I am not above them. I want them to know that I will get down in the dirt and work with them—side by side. They know that I don't consider myself any better than they are, and because of that, every day they give me an honest day's work."

I look over at Carlos who has a grin on his face, the look of genuine satisfaction. "Why did you stop boxing?" I ask.

"Ah, good question," he says. "I injured my shoulder in the Golden Gloves Championship." Carlos downshifts the two-ton as we stop at a traffic light. Then, he looks over at me and says, "Growing up, I thought I was invincible—that I would never get hurt. I thought I could box forever. It was after that championship bout that I realized that boxers have a short lifespan." The light turns green, and Carlos pops the clutch into first gear. He says, "When I was about your age, I started working for a landscaping company, and I was fortunate that the owner taught me the business side of things. After I won the Golden Gloves Championship, I took my winnings and my sponsorship money and bought a pick-up, a one-ton, and a two-ton. I also purchased the two buildings that make up my shop. I have very little overhead, and I have good workers." Carlos slides the stick shift into fourth gear, and a small smile appears on his face.

Looking at Carlos, I can't help but admire what he had literally built with his own two hands, both in the ring and as a landscaper.

Back at the shop, everyone helps in the process of putting the tools away. It's the same organized approach that I witnessed in the morning. Everyone working together. Everyone pulling his weight.

When everything is put away, Nate, Tommy, and Alvin jump in their cars and pull out of the parking lot in front of the shop.

Carlos stops me and says, "If you have a minute, there is something I would like to show you."

We walk from the main office building to a red brick building next door. Carlos uses his key to open the door. When he flips on the light, an entire gym comes into view. To my right, there is a heavy bag and a speed bag. To the left, there are weight benches, and curl bars. And right in the middle of it all is a full-sized, real-life boxing ring. It has bright red ring ropes, and the apron around the ring is also a bright red. A giant picture of two golden boxing gloves sits in the middle of the black canvas that is the floor of the ring.

"I thought you said you were out of the fight business," I say.

Carlos smiles and says, "You can't completely give up things that are in your blood." Carlos motions for me to follow him around the gym. He walks over to the speed bag, and soon his hands are flying like a windmill, striking the bag perfectly each time. He ends with one last powerful punch.

All I can say is, "Wow."

Carlos says, "Tomorrow is Sunday, and we don't work on Sunday. But I liked the way you worked today. You never let up. I will come in tomorrow and begin showing you how to box. We will train on Sunday, and then during the week, you can work on the skills that I taught you. Once the summer work gets going full speed, I will not have time during the week to work with you. You're going to have to work on your own. You can have access to this gym anytime you want."

I nod my head, realizing that Carlos was willing to share his most prized possession and also to work with me on his day off. "Why did you agree to help me?" I ask.

Carlos says, "I was about your size growing up. I dealt with some similar things. I know it's not easy. Besides, I think I can help."

When I wake up the next day, every muscle in my body hurts. I ease myself out of bed and take a quick shower. After a bowl of Wheaties, I head down to the shop. Carlos is already waiting for me.

He doesn't bother to say hello. In the gym, like his landscaping company, Carlos is all business. "We'll start with some sit-ups and push-ups. Twenty of each."

The sit-ups are easy. We do them in gym class. I struggle to get through all twenty push-ups, especially after yesterday's mulch-a-rama.

"Grab those gloves over there on the counter, and then come on over to the heavy bag," says Carlos, holding the bag with both hands. "A good boxer always protects his hands." After wrapping my hands, he looks around the heavy bag at me. "All right, let's see what you've got."

After sliding the gloves on, I stand in front of the bag feeling uncertain about what to do, and I feel completely out of place.

"Well, go ahead. Throw a punch," says Carlos.

I throw a half-hearted punch at the bag.

Carlos shakes his head and with more force in his voice says, "Like you mean it!"

My next punch has more velocity, but the bag deflects the punch.

Carlos shakes his head and raises his voice again. With a heavy accent, he says, "Pretend this is the boy who has been giving you such a hard time at school!"

My fists clench inside the boxing gloves as I think about Danny and Joey, and the next punch explodes into the bag.

"Now we're talking! It's not great, but it's better than what you started with," says Carlos. "Now, stand at an angle. Bend your knees. Don't just use your arm and shoulder. The punch should come from the ground up. Generate the punch from your feet through your legs and your waist. Explode into the bag. Always with passion!"

Taking his advice, I focus on generating my punch from my feet, through my waist, and throw another punch. Everything feels stronger, more solid.

Before I can celebrate my first good punch, Carlos barks instructions. "Keep your hands up. Protect your face. The right cross is a power punch. When you bring your fist back, bring it straight back. Don't ever drop your hands. Again."

Keeping my hands up, I throw another right cross into the bag, concentrating on generating the punch from the ground up and then bringing my fist straight back.

"Good! Again!" Carlos shouts. "This time with the left!"

Switching my legs around, I throw a left cross. The punch weakly glances off the bag.

"That's okay," says Carlos. "You must develop both hands. And the jab."

For the next half hour, we work on right and left crosses, and right and left jabs. After the first half hour, Carlos says, "Twenty more sit-ups and twenty more push-ups. Do all twenty, even if you can't do them in a row."

I drop to the mat and do the twenty sit-ups. It takes me three sets to get to the twenty push-ups. Ten, seven, and then three.

"Back to the heavy bag," Carlos instructs.

After two hours, 100 sit-ups, and 100 push-ups, and about 1,000 crosses and jabs, I can barely lift my arms.

"This week every day. Same routine," says Carlos, wiping some sweat from his brow. His intensity is unmatched.

"Yes, sir," I say, mostly because I am afraid to give Carlos any other response.

"Next week, you'll learn how to combo the jab with the cross. Then we'll get into the hook and the upper-cut, and then you'll learn some other two and three-punch combinations."

Even though I'm exhausted, I feel great. And I am grateful that Carlos has taken the time to help me. One thing I know for sure is that I don't want to be bullied any more. "Carlos," I say, "thank you for helping me."

Carlos nods his head. "It's my pleasure. We'll see you tomorrow. We have a busy summer ahead of us." Carlos walks over to a table in the gym and grabs his warm-ups and something else off the table. "One more thing," he says, handing me a book. "I want you to read this."

Looking at the cover, it reads: *The Power of One.*

Knowing that Carlos is not one for debate or lengthy explanations, I take the book and say, "Yes, sir."

The next day starts my summer of hard work and learning how to box. Each day, Tommy, Alvin, Nate, myself, and sometimes Carlos, go to a new job site. We plant trees, put down mulch, and plant flowers. We build tie walls and construct water gardens.

On the Friday of that first week, Nate and I build a brick sidewalk in front of an elderly lady's house. Alvin, Tommy, and Carlos go off to work on a water garden.

We start by digging seven inches down from the lady's front stoop to the sidewalk. We put down four inches of base gravel, and then one inch of leveling sand. The brick pavers take up the next 2 and ¼ inches. "Keep 'em coming," says Nate, as he straightens another red brick on top of the base of stone.

Handing Nate the brick I ask, "How did you end up working for Carlos?"

"Grew up with him in Youngstown. We've been friends since kindergarten. We both got in trouble when we cut each other's hair under one of the tables at school." Nate shakes his head and laughs at this. "Then we had a day where we set up a teepee outside the school. We must have been learning about Native Americans. We built a fire and everything. We ate our hot dogs raw. Every day it was something." Nate says this with a giant smile on his face.

Grabbing another brick off the crate I ask, "How long have you been working for him?"

"Dropped out of high school my senior year when my dad passed away to help support my family. I had six younger brothers and two younger sisters."

"You had a full house," I say.

Nate carefully positions another brick. "You could say that."

"What made you step up?" I ask.

"Before my dad died, he said that being a man is nothing more than being responsible for yourself and your family. I figured it was time for me to be a man."

While he tells me stories about his brothers and sisters, Nate and I work together in the hot Youngstown sun. I have to admit that I didn't get a good vibe from

Nate initially, but after getting to know him, and finding out about the sacrifices he made for his brothers and sisters, Nate earns my respect.

That week, each night, I start reading *The Power of One*. The story takes place in the 1940s, during World War II in South Africa. It's a story about a boy named Peekay, who gets picked on, but he meets a guy named Hoppie Groenewald, who teaches him about boxing. I start to get into the book because of the parts that are about boxing. I want to learn all I can about the sport.

The next Sunday, I have another two-hour session with Carlos. He teaches me the hook and the uppercut, and we work on two and three-punch combinations, from the left jab to the right cross to the hook and the uppercut. Slowly, my punches get stronger.

It is during my third week that Carlos drops Alvin and me off at a job. There are ten pine trees and two shovels. Carlos simply says, "I'll see you guys around lunch time."

Alvin and I literally dig in. Each hole needs to be twenty-four inches deep and just as wide. In the middle of all that digging, Alvin asks me, "How did you get hooked up with Carlos?"

"My dad does his accounting," I say.

Alvin drives the shovel into the soil and says, "Figured it was something like that."

"What about you?" I ask.

Alvin lets out a deep breath as he dumps the dirt on a pile next to the hole. "Served five years for aggravated burglary. Couldn't find no job. Not many people out looking to hire convicted felons."

"Five years?" I say with disbelief.

"Only served four because of good behavior, and now I'm on parole. Carlos took a chance on me. I'm not going to let him down."

"How did you survive in prison?" I ask.

"You toughen up quick. Or you die," he says, matter-of-factly.

We work in silence digging holes and throwing dirt. My imagination runs wild, picturing Alvin surviving in prison and what that must have been like.

"What you thinking about kid?" Alvin asks.

"Just couldn't imagine what that would be like," I say. "Being in prison."

"You don't want to. Just walk the straight and narrow. Work hard. Stay in school. Get that education. It'll keep you out of trouble."

"It seems like Carlos helps a lot of people out," I say.

"His philosophy is three strikes and you're out. He's a good man. Believes in giving people an opportunity to make good. No one else was willing to give me that chance, but Carlos did."

"What about Tommy?" I ask. "What's his story? He looks like he could play in the NFL."

"Funny you say that," says Alvin. "Tommy played Division I ball at Ohio State. Linebacker. A six foot three, two hundred and forty pound running back killer."

"What happened?" I ask.

"Tommy's got a temper. Got in a fistfight with the linebacker coach at OSU and got kicked off the team. Then he got himself into all kinds of trouble after that, went straight downhill. Had too much time on his hands. Started drinking and doing drugs. Then he started dealing drugs on campus. Got busted. He's got a record like me. Couldn't find work no-how." Alvin grabs the tree and maneuvers it next to the hole. "Grab that ball," he says, "and we'll slide it in. On the count of three. One, two, three."

I pull on the metal wire that surrounds the ball of dirt, and the tree drops into the hole.

"Cover her up," says Alvin.

I straighten the tree, and then I back fill the dirt into the hole and over the ball. "How long has Tommy been here?" I ask.

"Hmm," says Alvin, "going on three years now. I been here five. And Nate, I think he's been with Carlos since he started the company." Alvin pauses for a moment. "Tommy got his second strike about a year ago, arguing with a customer. Carlos said he better walk a straighter line."

I look around and see that we have two trees planted, still eight more to go. I think about Danny and Joey and how it was them thinking they're bad asses that brought me to this place, working with guys who have done time. Funny thing… so far it's been the best summer of my life.

After planting all the trees, lunch, and a quick mulch job, Carlos picks up Alvin and me. On the way back to the shop, Carlos is quiet. I can tell that something is bothering him. Plus, we haven't even worked a full day yet. We rarely call off early.

When we get back to the shop, Carlos walks over to Tommy, who is standing by his car. After about a minute, Tommy, the mountain of muscle, turns away. He is crying. His hands are shaking, and the tears are rolling down his face that is twisted up with pain.

"Don't do this, boss," he says.

"You knew the rules, Tommy," says Carlos. "I can't have you acting the way you do and representing my company. Can't do it. Won't do it. I gotta let you go."

"I'm sorry, boss. I'm sorry," is all Tommy can say. Without any further discussion, Tommy gets into his beat up, rusted-out car and pulls out of the parking lot.

"What happened?" asks Alvin.

Carlos shakes his head. "Another argument with a customer, and then he "bumped" into the customer." Carlos uses the quote signs with his fingers when he says bumped. "Tommy doesn't just bump into anybody. You know when he bumps yuh. Three strikes and you're out," says Carlos. "We're going to quit early today."

I can tell that firing Tommy was difficult for Carlos.

On the car ride home, I think about Tommy and wonder where he will go and what he will do for work. The job Carlos gave him was all that he had.

Summer rolls by, day after day and week after week. Each night I read a little bit more about Peekay and his journey in *The Power of One*. He continues to learn how to box, and he learns eight punch combinations. I want to learn like Peekay. In a way, he has become my hero. Not to mention, I have to read a book for my summer reading for school. Nothing like killing two birds with one stone.

I start going into the shop before the workday starts so I can train and work on the new punches and the new combinations, and Carlos agrees to meet me. Carlos tells me that my speed will make up for my size, so we work on footwork and combination after combination. He throws punches at me: thousands of hooks, jabs, and uppercuts. He teaches me how to duck the punches and protect myself by blocking the punches. He teaches me how to counter punch with combinations, telling me that the best combinations are the ones that land. During the summer, I hit a growth spurt and shoot up three inches and put on twenty pounds. I'm stronger and faster than I've ever been. Landscaping has given me muscles that I've never had before. Plus, with all the work in the gym with Carlos, I feel like I'm not afraid of anybody. Part of me can't wait to see Danny and Joey.

The routine of the summer days landscaping and the weekends and afternoons of training in the gym fly by, and before I know it, summer is over and school begins.

The first day of school of my junior year starts off like that day of my sophomore year during the last week of school. Joey and Danny are directly behind me. Only this time, my car doesn't stall. It was all that practice this summer of driving the one-ton and two-ton pickup trucks. When I pull into the parking lot, Danny pulls in right next to me. *Here we go,* I think to myself.

Danny pulls open my car door, but this time, when I step out of the car, Danny backs up a bit. I'm not the same kid I was just two and half months ago. Even though we still don't see eye to eye, he can see that I am bigger and stronger. And there's something more to me.

But Danny reaches down and gathers some of his confidence, maybe believing that things will continue as they were before. Danny says, "Where you been hiding all summer, Samantha?"

"Screw you," I say.

Without hesitation, Danny winds up and throws a right hook. It's the same punch I've seen from Carlos a thousand times over the summer. Instinctively, I raise my forearm and block the punch. Without flinching, I close my car door.

Looking at Danny with an angry stare, I say, "Strike one."

The look of shock on Danny's face is worth every single early morning workout with Carlos, every single push-up, sit-up, and combination. Every wheelbarrow of mulch, every tree we planted, and every weight I lifted, has prepared me to stand up against Danny.

The school day is just like any first day. Teachers review the year and pass out textbooks in class. Before lunch, Danny pushes me from behind, and my shoulder rams into my locker. I let out a deep breath and turn and say, "Strike two."

By the end of the day, I know the showdown with Danny Amato is coming. And the truth is, I can't wait. It's the moment I've been waiting for since the tormenting began in 8th grade. Like Carlos, I have decided to give Danny three strikes. He is down 0-2 in the count. And frankly, it doesn't look good... for him.

At the end of the day, I walk out to the school parking lot, and as expected, Danny is waiting by my car with Joey close by.

The banana is smeared all over the windshield, and I spot it on the door handle.

"Want a banana?" asks Danny, laughing to the crowd that is beginning to gather.

Strike three, I think to myself.

After I lower my backpack to the ground, a crowd of students starts to form an expectant circle. The strange thing is I don't hear anything. All I can see is the face of Danny Amato. My focus is so intense, so clear, that everything disappears around me, and from that moment, everything seems to move in slow motion.

It's as if I'm back in the gym with Carlos.

My focus has shifted to the fight.

Danny charges me like an angry bull, and I slide out of the way like a matador. He turns and charges again. This time I slip in an uppercut to Danny's gut, and he lets out a loud groan.

I slide on the balls of my feet, moving lightning fast. Danny keeps charging, and each time, I catch him with a jab or cross and move quickly away.

Soon, blood flows from Danny's mouth. He's breathing hard, and I can see in his eyes that he knows his fight is growing desperate.

The crowd of students has circled in closer. It's a primitive scene.

For me, this is what I've been waiting for.

The moment is mine. I've never felt more alive. The students want more blood, and that's exactly what they are going to get. When I think of Peekay and *The Power of One*, I think about the advice he received about acting from his head and not from his heart. I can't let my emotions get the best of me.

Danny abandons the charging tactic and instead, he tries to box me, which plays right into my hands. He misses with a right jab, and just like Carlos taught me, I envelope him in a six and then an eight punch combination. My fists are everywhere at once.

Danny staggers and stumbles.

My final right cross catches him square in the jaw, and he goes down face first on the blacktop, hard.

I roll Danny over. The blood flows from his mouth and nose. Turning his head, I look into his eyes, which are distant now. All the years of rage boil up inside me, but I don't shake at all. It's a steady calm. I pull back for the final punch, the decisive blow.

But before I land the haymaker, I think about Nate, Alvin, and Carlos. I think about Tommy. I think about the person I have become from my experience over the summer working side by side with those guys.

I have defended myself, but there is something else. I am above Danny Amato. Throwing the final punch would make me not unlike him.

Instead of throwing that final punch, I stand up and make my way through the crowd of students, walking to my car.

A path respectfully clears out of my way. Out of the corner of my eye, I see Sarah Stevenson. And for once… she notices me.

Without saying anything, I have made a statement, and I have a feeling that Danny won't be looking to bother me anymore.

Picking up my backpack, I open my car door and slowly climb into the front seat. The car starts right up, and I drive away from the stunned silence.

 **Questions on *Fighting Back*:**

1. An idiom is an expression that includes additional meaning. An example of an idiom would be, "Fixing that flat tire was a piece of cake." This is an expression meaning it was easy to do. Read the passage below from the short story *Fighting Back*. Determine the meaning of the idiom, and then, explain what context clues you used to determine the meaning of the idiom.

> Summer rolls by, day after day and week after week. Each night I read a little bit more about Peekay and his journey in *The Power of One*. He learns to box and learns eight punch combinations. I want to learn like Peekay. In a way, he has become my hero. Not to mention, I have to read a book for my summer reading for school. Nothing like killing two birds with one stone.

1. What is the meaning of the idiom, *killing two birds with one stone*?

a. To take out two birds with a stone
b. To throw a stone at two birds
c. To complete two activities with one action
d. To complete two tasks with two actions

1a. What context clues did you use to determine the meaning of the idiom: *killing two birds with one stone*?

_____

_____

_____

_____

_____

_____

2. A static character is a character that does not change over the course of a story. Pick a character in the short story *Fighting Back*. Explain why this character is static.

_____

_____

_____

_____

_____

_____

_____

_____

_____

_____

3. *Fighting Back* includes a story within a story. *Fighting Back* includes the novel, *The Power of One*. Research the novel, *The Power of One*, and then explain how the novel reflects the events in the short story. How does this change the depth of the short story? Include your research on the lines below, and then write your response on a separate sheet of paper.

_____

_____

_____

_____

_____

_____

_____

_____

_____

_____

_____

_____

_____

_____

_____

_____

_____

AUTHOR'S NOTE

Sports have played a pivotal role in my life. Sports have taught me important lessons about how to face adversity. It has been in the most difficult times in my life that I have turned to what I have learned on the football field, the basketball court, and on the track to get through those difficult times. I still think about the lessons coaches would preach: "Don't ever give up." "It's too easy to quit." "Rise to the occasion." "Don't stop until the whistle blows." "There is no shame in losing, only in the failure to make the most of an opportunity." "Play hard; play fair." "Do what's right." The list goes on and on. My experiences through sports have taught me how to be a leader, how to be a team player, how to never give up, and how to play the game until the final whistle blows. From middle school coaches, to high school coaches, to the coaches I had in college, there were always profound lessons about how to live my life. I'm hoping that these nine short stories not only entertain you, but my true hope is that you take away the idea that sports can teach you so much about yourself and the skills you will need to not only persevere in life, but how to thrive in everything you do, as a student, as an athlete, and as a human being.

AUTHOR BIOGRAPHY

Len Spacek has been a teacher and coach for over twenty-five years. Len wrote *Game On!* to entertain readers with action-packed short stories about sports, but he also wrote the stories so that athletes could see that sports can help them deal with the adversity they face in life as well. Len has coached numerous sports, giving him an insider's perspective on the nuances of each game. He has played competitively at the high school level in football, basketball, baseball, and track, and he competed at the collegiate level in football. He earned his undergraduate degree from the University of Dayton, his Master's Degree from John Carroll University, and his MFA in Creative Writing from the Northeast Ohio MFA program. His first novel was *The Final Play*.

Visit his website at lenspacek.com

Made in the USA
Middletown, DE
08 July 2022